Daniel Clarke Eddy

Our Travelling Party in Paris and Amsterdam

Daniel Clarke Eddy

Our Travelling Party in Paris and Amsterdam

ISBN/EAN: 9783743319776

Manufactured in Europe, USA, Canada, Australia, Japa

Cover: Foto ©ninafisch / pixelio.de

Manufactured and distributed by brebook publishing software (www.brebook.com)

Daniel Clarke Eddy

Our Travelling Party in Paris and Amsterdam

OUR TRAVELLING PARTY

IN

PARIS AND AMSTERDAM.

BY
DANIEL C. EDDY.

ILLUSTRATED.

BOSTON:
D. LOTHROP & COMPANY,
FRANKLIN ST., CORNER OF HAWLEY.

NOTE.

The author is pleased to find that the first two numbers of this series of books meet with an appreciation beyond his expectations.

The next number — "The Baltic to Vesuvius" — will take our travellers through the countries of Central Europe, into Italy. They will spend the winter in Rome, and journey northward in the early spring, meeting the storm of battle on the plains of Lombardy in midsummer.

CONTENTS.

CHAP.		PAGE
I.	LANDING AT CALAIS.	11
II.	PARIS FROM THE TRIUMPHAL ARCH.	23
III.	RIDE ALONG THE BOULEVARDS.	39
IV.	FROM THE MORGUE TO PERE LA CHAISE.	59
V.	GLIMPSES AT FRENCH ROYALTY.	75
VI.	PARIS BY SUN LIGHT AND GAS LIGHT.	95
VII.	THREE WAYS FOR SUNDAY.	121
VIII.	VERSAILLES AND THE COUNTRY.	135
IX.	THE BELGIC CAPITAL.	149
X.	THE FIELD OF WATERLOO.	162
XI.	VIEWS FROM ANTWERP STEEPLE.	183
XII.	FUN IN ROTTERDAM.	204
XIII.	MEMENTOS OF THE PILGRIMS.	223
XIV.	THE CITY ON LEGS.	241

ENGRAVINGS.

	PAGE
THE GATES OF DELFT.	2
JOHN ROBINSON'S PRAYER.	10
PARIS UNDER GROUND.	47
THE PRESENTATION.	91
SCENE ON THE BOULEVARDS.	107
THE NEW DEPOT.	137
THE CATHEDRAL OF BRUSSELS.	157
THE CHURCH.	213
DELFT-HAVEN.	226
PILGRIM COSTUME.	247
THE DUTCHMAN FISHING.	255

JOHN ROBINSON'S PRAYER.

PARIS TO AMSTERDAM.

Chapter I.

LANDING AT CALAIS.

IN England the American traveller feels at home. The people speak a language with which he is familiar; the habits and customs, the religious observances, the social developments, resemble the styles of life seen in his own land. His sympathies move on with the steady march of English ideas, and constantly he finds something to remind him of the great nation on the other shore of the broad Atlantic.

But when he crosses that narrow channel, and steps out upon the continent, he feels that he is among strange people, in a land of strange customs. The language of the inhabitants is unintelligible jargon; the form of government is repulsive to his republican prejudices; the features of common life differ widely from any thing he sees at home, and he is ever conscious that he is a stranger in a strange land.

Thus it was with the travellers whom we have followed across the Atlantic, through Ireland, Scotland, and England. The gentlemen were but imperfectly acquainted with the French language; Walter had studied it but a single term, while little Minnie could not understand a word of it.

They reached Calais late at night, and beneath a cloudy, moonless sky, stumbled ashore, Mr. Tenant holding Walter firmly by the hand, and Mr. Percy taking care of Minnie. At the landing they met several soldiers, and five or six armed policemen; one of whom shouted hoarsely as our friends came up,—

"Passports! passports! passports!"

"What does he want, pa?" asked Minnie.

"He wants our passports."

"What for?"

"To examine them, to see who we are, where we are from, and what we want."

So Mr. Percy took charge of the children, and Mr. Tenant went with the passports into a large room, where several men were sitting with piles of papers before them. They examined the documents very hastily, and gave them back again; and the party passed through the building, which in the darkness of the night they could not inspect, not knowing whether it was a police office, custom house, or depot, and found the cars on the other side, and were soon on their way for Paris.

The cars were very comfortable, and our travellers were able to get asleep. They had a whole carriage to themselves, and as the seats were sumptuously cushioned, and the road a very smooth one, they were as much refreshed as if they had been in a hotel. Minnie was the first one to awake; and as she rubbed her eyes, she said, with a yawn,—

"I say, Walter."

"What?"

"It is morning."

"Well — yes."

"We ought not to lose our views of the country," said Mr. Percy, letting down the window near him, and looking out.

"We have all slept soundly in this car, which is fitted up with as much elegance as a lady's boudoir," remarked Mr. Tenant, who was gazing about.

They conversed in an easy, desultory manner for some time, riding by villages, near vineyards, and along through a fine country, rarely making any stops. As the day advanced, the party felt the need of refreshments, and Walter said, —

"The first depot we come to, I will get something to eat, if the cars stop."

"We would hardly trust you out of our sight," replied his father.

"You would want a *valet-de-place* to help you buy your breakfast, Walter," said Mr. Tenant.

"A valet-de-*place!* What is that?" cried Minnie.

"Walter will tell you."

"Well, Walter, what is it?"

"A servant, I believe. But I should not need him. Pa, shall I try when we stop again?"

"Try what?"

"To purchase some refreshments?"

"Yes, my son, if you will keep within sight of us."

"All right, sir."

Just then the cars stopped at a place about fifty miles from Paris, and Walter sprang out, and hurried into the depot, and soon returned, bringing in a piece of paper a number of sandwiches, French sausages, and other specimens of French cookery.

"How did you make the change, Walter?" asked his father.

"Why, I gave him some English money, and he would not take it. Then I took out the five franc piece you gave me yesterday, and let him make his own change."

"Have you the right change back?"

"I don't know."

"A pretty boy to buy things. I'll try next time," shouted Minnie.

"Well, he gave me some small pieces, and I did not know what they were, and so hurried back as quickly as I could."

"Well, let us see what you have got," said Mr. Tenant.

So Walter displayed the articles he had bought, and soon they had made a hearty breakfast. The conversation turned on French cookery, and Minnie declared that she should be delighted with it, and indeed with every thing French.

"Ah, Min, you will not know what you do eat over here — whether frogs or dogs," said Walter.

"Hum! frogs and dogs!"

"Well, I have heard of the delightful manner in which French cooks serve up dogs, cats, and frogs, so that the most experienced will hardly distinguish them from the choicest dishes ever craved by the appetite of the epicure."

"Nonsense! ain't it, Mr. Tenant?"

"I do not know, child, how it is here; but I have heard the story of a distinguished American, who, in China, sat down to a sumptuous feast, and ate voraciously of a delicate dish which was set before him. When his dainty meal was finished, and he sat wondering what the food could be which had tempted his appetite to such an extent, a servant entered, and, wishing to have his curiosity gratified, and yet being entirely unacquainted with the language, he pointed to the dish, and said, 'Quack, quack,' meaning to ask if it was duck. The servant replied, 'Bow wow, bow wow,' intimating that the delicious food was not duck, but dog."

Just at that moment Minnie had a sandwich to her lips, and with an exclamation of disgust, she threw it out of the window, much to the amusement of her friends, who teased her a little for her admiration of French cookery.

"Minnie," said her father, "what we eat is much a matter of taste."

"How so, pa?"

"Why, we laugh at the French for eating frogs —"

"Ugh!"

"Yet we eat many things not as delicious."

"Delicious! How you talk!"

"Have you ever tasted turtle soup, Minnie?"

"O, yes, many a time."

"And how do you know the frog is not as good? and as clean?"

"Well, I declare!"

"In some countries dogs are eaten, and we think it very disgusting; yet we kill the filthy hog, and deem his flesh excellent."

"I am glad frog is not my taste."

"And who can say that your taste is better than that of the dog-eating Russian, or the frog-eating Frenchman?"

"I don't know, pa, but I wish Mr. Tenant would help me argue it."

A hearty laugh greeted the little girl, who felt some disposition to pout, but wisely concluded to laugh with the rest, at her own discomfiture.

"But, pa," said she, "this conversation annoys me — talking about frogs and dogs for food!"

"I know it does, my dear child; and I introduced it for a special reason."

"What was it?"

"I wished to show you that many things are mere matters of taste. You are now in a strange country, and will see many strange and unusual things. Your first impulse will be to condemn them because you have never seen them before. I wished to impress upon you the idea, that in much you will see, the difference is not so greatly in your own favor."

"I will think of that."

"Do so, and remember that you must not condemn what you see because it does not accord with your taste. Perhaps the taste of the people around you is best, after all; and you should be thoughtful ere you venture your opinion in condemnation."

"Thank you, pa, for the caution. I will endeavor to look at things on both sides."

The forenoon was half gone when the train reached Paris. The baggage of our travellers, which had been ticketed through from London, and thus escaped an examination at Calais, was here overhauled. A very civil, polite officer asked the children to unlock their bags, which they did, and he merely laid his hand upon the top, and passed on. The two gentlemen were not so fortunate, for a consequential personage persisted in taking out their clothing, and unrolling the packages, at which they were quite indignant, as the operation seemed to be unnecessary.

On entering a carriage, they drove to Hotel Meurice, in Rue de Rivoli, and were soon accommodated with a suit of elegant and spacious apartments, overlooking the garden of the Tuileries. Minnie's room opened into her father's, and Walter's into that of Mr. Tenant; and the view from all of them was very pleasant.

A little circumstance occurred just after their arrival which amused them very much. Breakfast was ordered, though it was late in the forenoon; and Minnie, who completed her toilet before the others, ran down before them. The building being very large, the windings numerous, and the passages long, she lost her way, and became somewhat bewildered, until she could not tell where to go. At length a very fine-looking gentleman came along the passage, and she appealed to him.

"Sir, can you tell me the way to the dining room?"

The man looked at her in astonishment.

"*Monsieur*, (sir,) I mean, where is the — the *déjeûner* (breakfast) room?"

The man smiled, and shook his head.

"Can't you understand me?"

The man shook his head.

Minnie thought again for some French word that she had heard Walter repeat, and then stammered out, "*La table, monsieur?*" (the table, sir.)

The man shook his head again; and finally, seeing her look at his jewelled watch chain, pulled out his watch, and thinking she might wish to know the hour, said, —

"*Il est midi,*" (it is twelve o'clock.)

"Hum! Stupid!" said the child to herself.

Just now Walter came along, and relieved Minnie of her embarrassment, by asking, very properly and in tolerable French, the way to the dining room, which they soon found, Walter indulging in a pleasant, good-natured laugh at Minnie's use of the language of which she scarcely knew a word.

When they were seated at the table, they found that the servants could all speak English, that the food was cooked in English style, and that the house had every appearance of an English hotel. This made them feel at home, and their anticipations of a delightful time increased as the day wore on.

The children were amused with every thing they saw. The streets, the people, the houses, were all so different from those seen in London, that they could not restrain their exclamations of pleasure and surprise. As they sat at their windows, they saw crowds of people on the sidewalks below; soldiers were marching along the streets; the *gendarmes* were standing on the corners, or moving about among the masses; the garden of the Tuileries across the street was thronged with happy men, women, and children, who were lounging on seats, walking under the trees, drinking beer at the stands, or engaged in some kinds of amusement.

Walter and his sister did not go out that evening, but rested for the work before them on the following days. They spent the evening in writing letters to friends at home. Walter penned a long letter to his mother, in which he told her all he had seen since he last wrote, what adventures he had met, what curious incidents had transpired, and all the news he could think of. Minnie wrote to Charlie a very curious letter, full of fun and nonsense, just like herself, over which Charlie doubtless had many a laugh when he read it.

They also found letters for them at the hotel, from home; and that well-known handwriting, from that dear mother, was read again and again, blotted with tears, and finally kissed, as a precious memento of fond maternal love. That night they slept sweetly — those honest, truthful, intelligent children, across whose young lives no shadow had ever yet fallen, and whose guileless hearts knew no great and sorrowing sin, and who, though young, trusted devoutly in the great God, whom they daily addressed — "Our Father, who art in heaven."

How beautiful the trusting confidence of children who can lie down to sleep, dreaming of no injury or danger, because they meditate no injury to others! no visions but happy ones flitting through the night-watch, because they only think of ministering to the happiness of others. The more we come in contact with the heartless world, its great wrongs, its amazing sorrows, its corroding cares, the more do we lose what always we might wish to keep — the trust and unsuspecting confidence of childhood.

Chapter II.

PARIS FROM THE TRIUMPHAL ARCH.

THE morning after their arrival in Paris, Walter, rushing into his father's room before sunrise, cried out, "*Bon jour, Monsieur,*" (good morning, sir.)

"Good morning, my son."

"I have ordered breakfast, and a carriage,— got a guide, and helped Mr. Tenant mark out the work for the day."

"Very well; I am glad of it."

"And my opinion was not consulted," cried Minnie, from the room adjoining.

"Of course not."

"Why not?"

"We set you down as a child, who had no opinion."

"Hoity, toity! No opinion, indeed! We'll see!"

"Where do you propose to go first, my son?" asked Mr. Percy.

"Mr. Tenant thinks we had better take a view of the city from the Triumphal Arch."

"That would be wise."

So after breakfast they all left the hotel, and, passing along *Rue de Rivoli*, entered Place de la Concorde, famous in the history of Paris.

"O, what a beautiful place!" cried Minnie, in delight.

"See those fine fountains, pa, and that pillar, and those statues. I never saw so lovely a spot!" said Walter.

"What is that pillar, pa, that Walter is running up to?" asked Minnie, seeing Walter direct his steps towards the column to which she pointed.

"That," replied Mr. Percy, "is the Luxor Obelisk, an Egyptian shaft, at least three thousand years old, and which is covered with unread Egyptian characters. It was brought from Egypt during the reign of Louis Philippe."

"What are those great drawings I see on the base?"

"Those are engravings and diagrams of the machine by which it was raised to its present elevation."

"Was it much trouble to raise it?"

"Yes, it was a great work, and it is said that the engineer who had charge of the work felt the most extreme solicitude as to his success; and as thousands gathered to see the obelisk rise to its position, he moved among them with a charged pistol protruding from his vest, with which he had determined to commit suicide, if, by any accident, he should fail in his attempt."

"He must have been a foolish man to have meditated such a dreadful deed as that."

"Yes, a man must be dreadfully blinded, to commit suicide."

"How nobly it looks in the centre here!"

"It is in a very showy position, and stands where the guillotine stood in the time of the revolution, and where the wretched Louis XVI. and Marie Antoinette, and their unfortunate friends, met a dreadful fate."

"Please tell me about it, pa."

"The story is a long one, my child, and you must read it for yourself."

"Just enough for me to understand about these things."

"Well, Louis XVI. was king of France, and Marie Antoinette was his queen."

"Who was she?"

"She was the daughter of Francis I., Emperor of Germany, and Maria Theresa, his wife. She was married to the King of France, and in the revolution was executed on this spot, her husband having been executed previously."

"Was she a good woman?"

"Much too good for such a fate."

"Why did they kill her then?"

"Because the people thought she had influenced her husband to oppress them."

"Was it not a dreadful fate?"

"Yes, the beautiful queen was confined in the Conciergerie, where in a few weeks her head became prematurely gray, and—"

"What is the Conciergerie?"

"It consisted of a series of subterranean dungeons. The queen was taken from this horrid prison, and executed, October 14, 1793. She was carried to the place on a cart rude in structure, and hard to ride in. As she rode along, many of the women of Paris gathered around the cart, and reviled the fallen queen, crying out, 'Down with the Austrian! down with royalty!' As the poor creature was thrown about in the cart, unable to stand or sit, the wretches shouted in merriment. At length they arrived at this spot, just where they had killed her husband."

"Was she calm?"

"Yes; so it is said."

"How could she be?"

"Sometimes people who are naturally very timid have fortitude in times of such severe trial."

"Well, go on."

"There is but little more. She was taken from the cart to the scaffold, bound to the plank, and the axe descended. The head dropped into a basket placed for it, and the executioner caught it up, and held it aloft, while the people shouted coarsely, '*Vive la République!*'"

"Can you describe the guillotine to me, pa?"

"Some time at the hotel, or elsewhere, I will; not now."

"Had the queen any children?"

"Yes, a boy and girl."

"Poor, dear children!"

"One was the dauphin, seven years old."

"What became of them?"

"The young dauphin was killed probably by harshness and severity. Simon, his brutal jailer, had orders to get rid of him. He was neglected, half fed, and abused until his reason tottered; and he is said to have died June 9, 1795, in his tenth year."

"Is said to have died?"

"Some have questioned whether he died, or whether he was taken away, and carried to America. One or two persons have pretended to be the dauphin."

"What became of the princess?"

"The sister, Maria Theresa, named for her grandmother, was permitted to go to Austria. On the fall of Napoleon, after she had become a beautiful and gifted woman, and the Duchesse d'Angoulême, she returned to France, lived a checkered life, and died not long ago somewhere in Germany."

"What a terrible tale is this!"

"You must read it all carefully. You will find it to equal in thrilling interest the sad tale of Mary, Queen of Scots."

"Where can I find it?"

"When you return home I will obtain the account in some instructive historical work, and you can read it."

Leaving this spot, so consecrated with blood, the theatre of so many terrible scenes, the party entered the Elysian Fields.

"What place is this, father?" asked Walter.

"This is the famous Champs Elysees."

"O, yes, I have heard of it."

They found the place a fine promenade, striking out from Place de la Concorde one and a quarter miles, laid out with foot and carriage paths, and forming a beautiful resort for the gay and fashionable crowds, who sit and walk by hours, hearing sweet music and witnessing gay scenes. Trees finely trimmed, and hedges carefully trained, give shelter from the sun, while thousands of chairs and benches furnish seats when the people are weary. These grounds are let for panoramic and other exhibitions, from which an income is derived of about twenty thousand francs per annum. On the afternoon or evening of any pleasant day, thousands of persons are seen moving about under the trees, or resting themselves on the benches, or enjoying some of the sports of the place and occasion.

"Why, pa, I should think it was a muster ground," said Minnie, as they entered the shaded walks.

"So should I," replied Walter.

The scene was a very interesting one. All kinds of amusements seemed to be in progress. Beneath the trees, young men, in large numbers, were engaged in the various games calculated to give strength and vigor to the muscular system. On both sides of the Avenue de Neuilly, which is twelve feet wide, and paved with bitumen, were pavilions richly decorated and finely illuminated, radiant with all the colors of the rainbow, and flowing with banners, ribbons, pennants, and laces. Some of these were open on one side, and filled with singers, and in others various fancy articles were exposed for sale. The party wandered about for some time, and then passed on towards the Triumphal Arch.

"From this Arch we shall get a fine view of the city," remarked Mr. Tenant, as they approached.

"Who built it, Mr. Tenant?" asked Walter.

"It was commenced by Napoleon, and completed in 1836, at a cost of more than ten million francs."

"It does not look as if it was so costly a structure."

"No, but we shall find, when we reach it, that it is very imposing. It consists of a grand central arch, ninety feet high and forty-five feet wide, through which passes a traverse arch, scarcely less bold and magnificent in its proportions."

"How high is it?"

"One hundred and fifty-two feet, and sinks its solid stone foundation twenty-five feet below the surface of the ground."

They reached the Arch, paid a woman a franc, and went up to the top.

"How many steps did you make, Minnie?" asked Walter.

"Two hundred and sixty."

"I counted two hundred and sixty-one."

"Grand, grand!" exclaimed Mr. Tenant, as he caught a view of the city.

"Eureka! Eureka!" shouted Walter.

And the view was indeed one of the finest in the world, and long they stood gazing down upon it. The Champs Elysees, with the spacious avenue, was thronged with people. Beyond, the palaces were glistening in the sun; old Notre Dame and the Pantheon lifted up their towers and domes, like monuments amid a sea of habitations; the ornamented columns pointed upward, like the fingers of a giant; the broad, flat roof of La Madaleine stretched out like a plain; while all around, a beautiful country was spread out in every direction.

"Pa, will you point out to us some of the objects of interest?" asked the children.

"Yes, after we have swept our gaze about, and taken a general view."

When they had stood some time looking out upon the sea of shining roofs and stately buildings, Mr. Percy said to the children, —

"Now I will tell you what prominent objects we can see, as near as I can from this map of the city I have in my hand."

"Well, father," said the lad, "Minnie and I have been wondering what that tall pillar is which we see yonder."

"O, that is near our hotel."

"What is it?"

"It is a pillar erected by Napoleon to commemorate his German victories. It stands in what is called Place Vendome."

"What is that figure on top?"

"That is the bronze figure of Napoleon himself, who is looking out from his dizzy elevation upon the passing multitudes below."

"Is it a very fine pillar?"

"Yes. It is an imitation of the Trajan Pillar at Rome, and surpasses it in grandeur, and in the heroism of the deeds which it commemorates."

"What is it made of?"

"It is made of stone, and covered with bronze bass-reliefs, formed entirely of cannon taken in the battles of the conqueror. The bass-reliefs are spiral, and display the most noted events in the German campaigns."

"And what is that dome I see out there, looking so nobly, as it rises above the flat roofs?"

"That is the dome of the Hotel of the Invalids, a building we shall visit in a few days, where we shall see many old soldiers."

Mr. Percy also pointed out the various objects of interest all over the city, a general view of which was obtained by each member of the party; and they all descended, having enjoyed themselves finely, and feeling fully repaid for the tiresome ascent.

At the base they found an old woman who had views of Paris to sell, and our party purchased several of them to take home to their friends. Walter took the roll of engravings under his arm, and they all went slowly down the broad and spacious avenue, looking at the people as they swept by, or gazing in at the windows upon the rich goods and rare articles displayed to view; and when they reached their rooms, the children were ready to throw themselves on their beds and rest.

In the afternoon of the same day, Mr. Percy said to Walter, —

"My son, I think you had better not go out again to-day."

"I do not wish to; I prefer to rest."

"How will you spend the time here?"

"In writing letters."

"Did you not promise Mr. Falkner, your teacher, that you would write to him?"

"Yes, sir, and I will do it to-day."

"That would be well, for Mr. Falkner has done much to improve your mind, and give you a thorough training in your studies as far as you have gone."

"I will write a long letter."

"Write it well; be careful of your sentences,

and show him how well you can write, and with what skill you can compose."

Mr. Percy and Mr. Tenant then went out, and Walter was left with Minnie as his charge. The little girl, however, preferred to have an afternoon nap, and Walter wrote the following letter to his school teacher : —

Paris, 1858.

Dear Sir:

I promised to write you during my absence, and I improve the present time to do so. We are now in one of the great cities of the world, and though we have had but a general and very imperfect view of it, I wish to state the impressions made on my own mind by what I have seen since we have been here.

Up to this time, our tour has been of the utmost interest to us all. We have seen many of those things which have long been partially familiar by our reading, and now we have come to scenes of new and strange fascination for us all.

The city of Paris is one of the most beautiful on the globe, in some respects excelling in the elegance of its public buildings, and the taste of its people, any other. London is the great mart of commerce. Every where are seen the evidences of industry, and the tokens of successful business. You do not think of looking for

VIEW OF PARIS.

beauty there; but every street and lane, thronged with hurrying, driving people, force upon you the conviction that you are in the world's great exchange, the vast market place of nations. You expect to be jostled, trodden upon, spattered with mud, lose your temper, and perhaps your purse. But Paris strikes you differently. The streets are wide and clean; the houses are neat and gay colored; the people are quiet, courteous, and gayety comes borne upon every blast. No two cities could present a more striking contrast, and in no two do the forms of life more widely vary, and appear more strikingly dissimilar.

Our first view of the place was from the Triumphal Arch. This is a magnificent monument erected by order of Napoleon, to celebrate his victories, and is one of the most imposing and elaborate structures of the kind in the world. It stands on elevated ground, on the outskirts, and overlooking the city. It is sixty feet front and twenty feet thick, and forty-five feet high. Father thinks that from the top of this Arch the most beautiful city view in Europe is obtained. On looking from the Golden Gallery of St. Paul's, in London, though the view is a very fine one, the houses are dingy and the streets irregular; the public buildings are so located as not to be seen with any great degree of distinctness, and over the whole hangs the perpetual London fog, obscuring the vision and spoiling the view. The prospect from the dome of St. Peter's, in Rome, father tells me, is very fine; but Rome is small in its extent, and one of course must conjure up the memories of the past, to give him an idea of the sublimity of the view he is taking.

But standing on the top of the Napoleon Arch, the whole city of Paris is spread before the eye in one direction, while in an opposite direction a most magnificent country is spread out for many miles around. Looking down from the Arch, the Elysee Avenue is before you, one and one fourth miles long, a magnificent street, with its sidewalks of bitumen, its rows of trees, and gas lights on both sides, and always filled with gay people, and splendid equipages, running through the Champs Elysees, and terminating in the Place de la Concorde, against which the Palace of the Tuileries fills the view. All over the city the streets and parks can be seen, not narrow and crooked, but straight and wide; the house-tops not covered with the red, dingy tiles, but clean and white; the public buildings rising distinctly, the palaces all in view, as if they were all located and placed to look towards the Arch on which you stand, doing homage to the mighty genius of Napoleon, which hovers over the work of his hands. The tower of the Invalides, the dome of the Pantheon, the Corinthian glories of the Madeleine, the antique outlines of the Louvre, and the curious forms of the many churches, are all clearly seen, while the very heavens, as if to shame the murky, humid atmosphere of its mighty rival London, are clear; the skies are bright, and not a vapor seems to float in the transparent atmosphere.

Descending from the Arch, we walk down the beautiful avenue to the heart of the city. The Arch leads into the Champs Elysees, one of the most noted places in Paris. It is a public pleasure ground, laid out in 1616, by Marie de Medicis, improved by the notorious Madame de Pompadour, and covers an area of several acres, beautifully laid out with streets, and set with trees, and furnished with the various facilities for out-of-door pleasure. Here every day, especially on the Sabbath, we are told, may be seen thousands of the gay Parisians, in all kinds of costumes, civil and military, whiling away the time with their children and friends. The grounds, about a hundred yards wide at one end, and seven hundred yards at the other, form the play ground and breathing place of the city, and the people crowd here in large numbers to enjoy themselves.

Thus I have endeavored to describe the first view we had of the city of Paris. When we have seen more, I will write you more. You must excuse my haste and brevity, and trust that I may make more improvement before I return to your school. I remain your pupil,

WALTER PERCY.

When his father returned, Walter had folded his letter, and, weary with his long walk in the morning, had fallen asleep, his head resting on the table. Minnie also was in the land of dreams.

Chapter III.

A RIDE ALONG THE BOULEVARDS.

THE next morning a carriage was taken, and the company entered it for a ride about the city.

"Where shall we go?" asked Walter.

"Let us ride along the Boulevards first," replied Mr. Tenant.

"What are the Boulevards?" asked Minnie.

"They are wide, fine streets, nicely paved, and having wide sidewalks. They are the favorite resort of promenaders, and all along them are rich stores."

"But why are they called 'Boulevards'?"

"Because these stores are on the foundation of the ancient fortified wall of the city."

"When was the wall demolished?"

"In 1670."

"Are the Boulevards — how do you pronounce it? — far distant?"

"The word is pronounced '*Boo'le-vär:*' we are just turning into Boulevard des Capucins."

"See the people sitting on the sidewalks, eating their breakfast out of doors," cried Minnie, as the carriage drove on.

"You will see much of that before we finish our ride."

"What shops are those I see?"

"They are the *cafés* you have often heard of, my child."

"But what is going on now, that they are all so full of people?"

"Probably nothing unusual. The Frenchman sometimes loves his coffee more than he does his home, and often spends more time in the *café* than in the bosom of his family. In these Boulevards, at almost any hour of the day or evening, may be seen scores and hundreds of men and women sipping coffee and eating ices in the open street. In front, as you see, are large numbers of little tables, with one or two chairs to each, each occupied, while within the *café* are busy waiters, hurrying to and fro, to receive orders and supply the wants of their patrons."

"How strange!"

"To us it is, but it is customary here. In some parts of the city, and along the Boulevards, as we shall see as we ride about, little arbors are fitted up with hanging lamps; fountains abound, and cool retreats, and hither resort hundreds to eat, drink, and enjoy. The enchantments which art throws around these fairy spots render them the favorite resorts of men of all classes and conditions. The visitor must purchase some article, or pay two or three sous for the use of the chair and table. Thus the keepers make good livings, and are enabled to embellish their premises in very gorgeous style.

"Here," said Mr. Tenant, "is the church we saw yesterday from the Triumphal Arch."

"What church?" asked Walter.

"The Madeleine."

"O, let us go in! — see, the doors are open."

They ascended the steps, and entered the noble structure, where they found many people bowing in various places, or gazing on the decorations, while at the altar were lights burning, and a priest bowing.

"O, how magnificent!" whispered Minnie.

"Very grand!" replied Walter.

"When was it built, pa?"

"In 1764 it was commenced, and finished in the time of Louis Philippe."

"Why did it take so long to build it?" asked Walter of his father.

"Because in the troublous times of France, the work was often suspended. Louis XV. originated it, and selected the designs of Constant d'Ivry. When Napoleon I. came to the throne, he determined to go on with the work, and instead of a church, convert it into a Temple of Glory."

They walked about this wonderful building, and the admiration of the children seemed to know no bounds. And indeed the Madeleine is well worthy of admiration. Few of the children who read this book have ever seen one half so beautiful. In form it is a parallelogram, — the meaning of which the young reader will see by turning to his dictionary, — and is finely lighted from the ceiling. The magnificent structure is built in the Grecian style of architecture, and cost the immense sum of thirteen million and seventy-nine thousand francs, or more than two million six hundred thousand dollars. It is three hundred and twenty-eight feet long, and one hundred and thirty-eight feet wide. It is surrounded by Corinthian pillars about fifty feet high and sixteen and a half in circumference. The light comes in through the ceiling, which is beautifully painted, and makes a very fine display.

When they had admired this church, they again entered the carriage and drove on. The day was beautiful, and the people were out in large numbers, and the Boulevards looked very gay and cheerful. At length they came to a place where several men were at work upon the sidewalk.

"What are they doing?" asked Minnie.

"Mending the sidewalk," replied her father.

"But the sidewalks are solid granite, and these men are at work with tar and gravel."

"Are you sure the sidewalks are granite?"

"Yes, sir, they were composed of granite in the Place de la Concorde, and the Avenue de Neuilly, and also in Rue Royale."

"But—"

"And it is granite here; and what are they putting on tar for?"

"You are too certain of the matter, my child. These sidewalks, that look so beautiful and form so fine a promenade, are not of granite, but of a sort of composition, made up of pitch and gravel, and which, being put on hot, soon hardens and becomes firm, thus making noble sidewalks at a very trifling expense. If you get out of the carriage and go and stamp your foot on it, you will find that the impression will be left on what you thought was granite."

Minnie sprang from the carriage, which was drawn up against where the men were at work, and with all her strength, stamped with her foot.

"Why, pa," she cried, "I have left the whole impression of the heel of my boot."

"I thought you could do so; the hot sun is acting on the pitch."

Minnie stood looking at the men, observing how quickly a square of several yards was covered over, and what a nice walk it made as soon as it hardened, and she came back to the carriage much pleased with what she had seen.

"Why don't they have such sidewalks in Boston?" she asked; "they would be so much finer than the hard, coarse, brick pavement."

"There are good reasons why they do not have such pavement in Boston."

"What are they?"

"Can you not guess?"

"No, I am sure I cannot."

"Can Walter?"

"I have been thinking."

"Well."

"I think, sir, that the frosts in winter would soon throw it all up, and crumble the walks to pieces, so that we should be obliged to lay them every spring."

"Yes, that would be so; such composition spread on our streets could not stand the severity of a New England winter."

"Go on, driver," cried the little girl.

The driver cracked his whip, and his horses started at a brisk rate, but soon fell into a gait little faster than a walk; but our friends did not wish to ride fast, so they were satisfied. As they went on looking at the people, the stores, the elegant carriages that passed them, and all the objects of interest, Minnie espied a man running on before them, with a long ladder on his shoulder; and while she was watching him, she saw him stoop down and open a trap door in the middle of the street, and putting his ladder down, descend over it, and drawing on the cover, leave the street as before.

"Well, I declare, that is funny!"

"What?" said Mr. Tenant.

"Why, didn't you see that man descend into the earth, just at the spot we are now riding over?"

"Yes; but what is there funny about that?"

"A good deal that is funny — where did he go to?"

"Perhaps he has gone down through to come out on the other side."

"Don't plague me, Mr. Tenant, but tell me."

"Well, child, there is an under ground and an above ground to Paris."

"A what?"

"A city above the surface, which you see, and —"

"A glorious one too."

"And one under ground, which you do not see."

"Tell us what you mean."

"I will tell you. Underneath the city are immense excavations, used for the purpose of drainage, water works, and bones from the cemeteries, and other useful purposes."

"Were the excavations made for these purposes?"

"No; they are much more extensive than they need be for this. They were probably made to get the stone of which the early buildings were erected."

"Are these street passages all there are?"

"No; many years ago a house called Tombe-Issoire, out on the old Orleans road, was bought for a grand entrance to the catacombs."

"How deep do they go down?"

"About seventy-seven steps."

"Whew!"

"How extensive are the catacombs?" asked Walter.

"From north to south they extend from Rue de l'Ecole de Medecine to Barriere Vaugirard, and out east they go to the Jardin des Plantes."

"Are the excavations arched?"

"Yes; but you will go down into them and see them, and judge for yourselves."

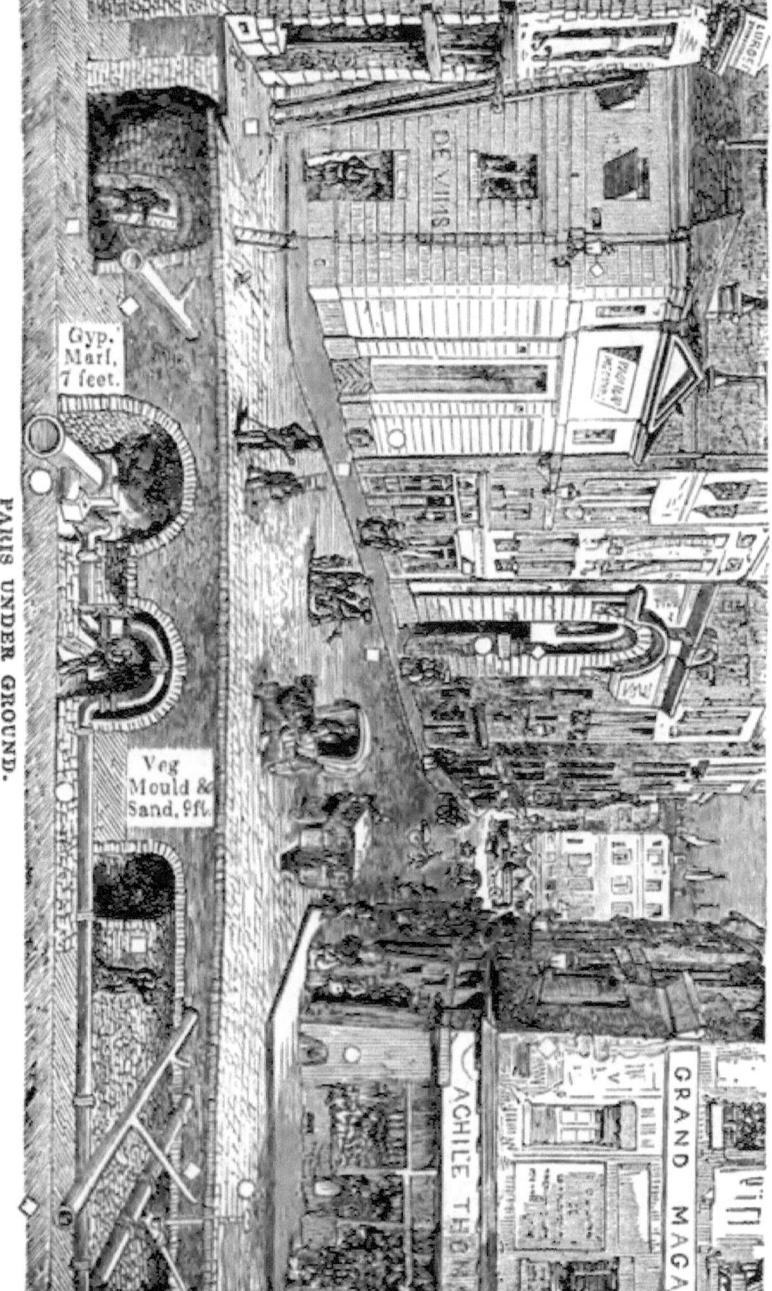

PARIS UNDER GROUND.

The young reader will find on the opposite page a good view of a section of Paris underground, which is as wonderful, if not as fascinating and beautiful, as Paris above ground.

As they advanced farther along, they met a carriage driving slowly, in which sat a venerable looking man in military attire, and at whose appearance the people seemed to be very enthusiastic. He was a noble looking man, and his breast was covered with sparkling ornaments.

"Who is he, father?" asked Walter.

"I do not know, my son."

"What were those ornaments on his breast?"

"One I suppose to be the Grand Cross of the Legion of Honor."

"I have often heard of it. What is it?"

"The Legion of Honor is an institution founded by Napoleon, which distributes honors to worthy men, civil and military."

"Please tell me more about it."

"Well, all nations have honorary titles to bestow on favorites. In England there are various orders, and it is esteemed a great distinction to have them conferred. Under the old regime in this country, there was the order of St. Louis, and the king bestowed the cross of the order on persons whom he deemed worthy. At the time of the revolution the order was abolished, and the cross was no more distributed. But Napoleon, understanding the weakness of men, and their desire for honors, determined to establish a new order, that should be connected with his own name. When the time came, Napoleon proposed it, and declared that the 'Legion of Honor' would be the commencement of the reorganization of France. Many of his court opposed it as a remnant of the old royalty. But the persevering emperor carried his purpose."

"I should like to examine the cross," said Minnie.

"Perhaps you will have an opportunity before we leave Paris. Here, Walter," continued Mr. Percy, handing his son a little book which he took from his pocket, "is an account of the inauguration of the order; read it aloud; it is interesting."

"Yes, sir," replied Walter. "Please, driver, walk the horses."

"*Oui,*" (yes,) replied that personage, who could understand a little English, but could not speak it.

Walter took the book, and read low but distinctly, so that all in the carriage could hear, and yet not so as to attract attention outside, the following statement of the establishment of the Legion of Honor: "On the 14th of July, 1804, at the very hour when the old constitution had fallen with the walls of the Bastile fifteen years before, the new one rose with the Legion of Honor. As the 14th fell on a Saturday, the ceremony was put off to the next day. It took place in the Chapel of the Invalides, where the ashes of the emperor now rest. After a grand review, the emperor arrived on horseback at the Invalides, coming through an innumerable crowd of eager observers. He ascended the throne in the choir. In a gallery opposite were the Empress Josephine and her daughter Hortense, who was afterwards married to Louis Bonaparte."

"O, I should like to have seen Josephine and Hortense!" broke in Minnie.

"Hush, child; let me read. 'Besides these, there were eighteen marshals of the empire, only four being away on the field of battle. After mass had been performed by Cardinal Caprara, and the gospel read, M. de Lacépède, of the Institute, the grand chancellor of the order, rose from his seat. Napoleon had resolved to honor intellect by placing him at the head of the Legion of Honor. Lacépède pronounced the inaugural discourse, and called over the names of the grand officers, who took the oath required by the statutes before the throne. Then the emperor delivered a speech such as none but he could deliver, and, reading the oath to the legionaries, asked them in a loud voice whether they would take it. All, with one voice, answered in the affirmative. Two large basins were brought, one of gold, containing the gold crosses for the officers, and the other of silver, containing the silver crosses for the simple members. The symbols and the device were the same for both classes: a number of standards collected together, the effigy of Napoleon, and the words 'Honor and Country,' borrowed from the old monarchy. M. de Ségur, grand master of the ceremonies, took a cross of each metal, and gave them to M. de Talleyrand Perigord, grand chamberlain; he passed them to Louis Bonaparte, constable of the empire, who placed them on the breast of Napoleon. At this moment, three rounds of applause reëchoed through the building. Then the distribution commenced. First came the members of the Institute, comprising all the most distinguished philosophers, literary men, and artists of the day, and headed by Monge, the very man who had previously ridiculed honorary distinctions as mere playthings. After these, the military officers of high rank received the new decorations at the hands of the emperor. A *Te Deum* by —.'"

"A what?" asked Minnie.

"A *Te Deum*."

"What is that?"

"It is a song of praise, to be sung in churches, I believe."

"But why is it so called?"

"I do not know. I often see it in print, and know that it means a song of praise. Perhaps father can tell us why it is so called."

Mr. Percy, on being appealed to, told them that the hymn of praise called *Te Deum* derived that name from its first words, "Te Deum laudamus." Thee, God, we praise.

"Read on, Walter."

"Don't interrupt me again. 'A *Te Deum*, by Lesueur, followed the distribution of the crosses; and in the evening there was a concert at the Tuileries, a general illumination of the city, and a grand display of fireworks on the Pont Neuf.

"'But the army not having been able to be present at the Invalides, Napoleon went to them at Boulogne, where a second *fête*, equal in splendor to the first, was celebrated. On the 16th of August, at ten o'clock in the morning, the emperor, in the simple uniform of the light horse, appeared in the camp on horseback, and took his seat in the bronze chair of Dagobert, which is still to be seen at the Museum of Sovereigns. From this elevated position he commanded a view of the harbor, the two camps, the batteries, the harbor of Vimeux, and the coasts of England. Salvos of artillery thundered forth, and the crosses were placed in helmet and cuirasses. At the sound of eighteen hundred drums, sixty thousand men began to march, and the legionaries, leaving their ranks, came one after the other to receive the cross from the hand of the emperor.'"

"Now, children," said Mr. Percy, "remember this account, and it will add interest to the cross when you see it sparkling on the breast of any one who has nobly earned it."

"I have heard of the 'Order of the Garter.' What is that, father?" asked Walter.

"That is an English order, instituted by Edward III."

"Why is it called the *Garter?*" asked Minnie.

"There are various accounts of the origin of the order. The most plausible one is that related on the authority of English historians, that the king one day found a garter belonging to the Countess of Salisbury, and displayed it before his courtiers, who smiled at it. The king, on seeing their smiles, replied, '*Honi soit qui mal y pense*,' which became the motto of the order, which he at once founded."

"What does that motto mean?"

"Evil to him that evil thinks hereof."

"Is this order reputable and influential?"

"Certainly; its knights are made from the princes and peers."

"Well, the origin is low enough."

"Many of these orders have low and frivolous origins, but they have great influence."

"What is the — the — sign of the order? — you know what I mean."

"The insignia?"

"Yes, sir."

"A garter, mantle, cap, George, and collar."

"What do they do with the garter?"

"It is worn by the knight on the left leg, between the knee and the calf."

"What does it look like?"

"Why, a garter, to be sure."

"How is it made?"

"I can hardly tell; but the motto is on it."

"Can you tell us about any other orders?"

"Yes, at some leisure time, I will tell you about several English, French, and Austrian orders. We had better now pay our attention to the Parisians; we can talk about the orders any time. We ought not to lose any of the benefit of our fine ride to-day."

"See, Walter, how many women there are in the streets with little night caps on," said Minnie.

"They are not night caps."

"What are they?"

"They are caps that are worn, father tells me, by the low classes of females to save the expense of bonnets."

"Well, they look queer."

"Because we are unaccustomed to the sight."

The reader probably knows that the streets of Paris, at all hours of the day, are filled with young women who wear a comfortable linen or muslin cap, instead of a bonnet; and after the odd look ceases to affect the mind, the costume seems to be very tidy and pretty. Minnie at length came to like it so well, that without making allowance for the difference of climate, she wished the Bostonians would adopt it. Indeed, she soon fell in love with all the Parisian forms and customs. She was determined to like every thing she saw in that beautiful city.

"Now," said Mr. Percy, "it is about time for us to return to the hotel. We have been driving about some time in the Boulevards, and I propose that we draw up at one of the *cafés*, and take some French coffee, and other refreshments."

" That is it," cried Minnie.

" Glorious idea," said Walter.

" I approve the plan," added Mr. Tenant.

The driver was directed to take them to a well-known *café* in the Boulevard des Italiens; and they all alighted at a well-furnished restaurant, where many gentlemen and ladies were sitting sipping coffee and other dishes.

" Now, Walter," said his father, " put your French in exercise, and see if you can get us what we want."

Walter thought a moment, and then uttered a most unintelligible sentence, in which *viande*, (meat,) *hibou*, (owl,) and *les gateaux*, (the cakes,) figured conspicuously.

The servant looked dolefully at the company; the gentlemen began to laugh; Minnie, understanding that Walter had made a mistake, clapped her hands.

" What did I say?" asked Walter, reproachfully.

" Say! You did not say much of any thing."

" What did I come nearest to saying?"

" You came nearest to ordering owl instead of chicken. Do not try to put it all in one sentence. Ask for articles separately."

Walter thought a moment, and then, looking at the servant, said,—

"*Café*," (coffee.)

"*Oui*," (yes.)

"*Hibou*," (owl.)

"No, no!" said Mr. Percy.

"*Dindon*," (turkey,) said Walter

"No, no!" said his father.

"*Poulets*," (chickens,) cried Walter, almost vexed.

"*Oui*," (yes,) said the servant.

Thus with considerable difficulty they obtained refreshments; and, having partaken of them, they all rode to the hotel, where, after resting a while, they went out and walked in the Champs Elysees, which they found filled with happy appearing people, in holiday attire.

Chapter IV.

FROM THE MORGUE TO PERE LA CHAISE.

THERE are two places in Paris that one cannot enter without a feeling of sadness. In one, the scenes witnessed repulse and disgust the spectator; in the other, the sadness is alluring, captivating, and inviting. One is a low, death visited building on the banks of the Seine; the other is a beautiful garden of graves on an eminence, from which the living city is full in view.

"What is the Morgue, pa?" asked Minnie, one morning as they were riding out.

"The city dead house, my child."

"Shall we see it?"

"Yes, we are riding in that direction. There it is, just before us."

On reaching the Morgue, the gentlemen, who knew something of the character of the place, endeavored to persuade Minnie not to go in; but she, determined to see all she could, persisted. The Morgue is the house where dead bodies, found in the river or streets, are brought to be identified by their friends, and few persons care to visit it a second time. There are two large rooms, separated by a partition of glass, in one of which the bodies are laid in view of those who gaze in from the other. The corpses are divested of their clothing, and laid on inclined tables of shining brass, so that the whole person, with whatever scars and marks, or other distinguishable things there may be about it, may be seen. The clothing is hung up over the body, that it may serve as a means of identification.

"Shall we see any bodies?" asked Minnie, as she held closely to Walter's hand.

"We will see soon," replied Walter, in a whisper.

They all drew near the window, and looked in, and the children, with a low cry of horror, sprang back and covered their eyes with their hands. Three ghastly corpses were there, and the terrible look had sent a cold chill all through their quivering frames.

"Come, let us go," said Minnie, drawing Walter away.

"Awful sight!" whispered Walter.

Of the three persons, the first was a fine, manly-looking form, a handsome countenance, which even in death was not destitute of attraction, but fearful sores covered the whole body, and rendered the spectacle as loathsome as if he had died of leprosy.

The second was a man about forty-five years old, who had been killed in some kind of fight. His face was bruised and blackened; his eyes seemed as if they had been nearly gouged out, and there were several stabs from which the blood was still oozing. The spectacle was hideous beyond description; and almost every one who looked on turned away aghast from that sad and sorrowful looking scene.

The third was a woman, about twenty-two years of age, fair and beautiful in the lasting sleep. She appeared to have been beaten to death; several wounds being visible on her person, her arms and shoulders bruised and blackened, and one side of her face gashed, as if with a sharp knife. Her dark hair lay back, leaving a fine forehead bare, and the clothes hanging over her indicated a person in comfortable circumstances.

"O brother, *do* let us go!" cried Minnie.

"Terrible sight, Minnie!" replied Walter.

"Come out, come out!"

"Hush, Minnie; you are drawing attention."

"Do come!"

They were all glad to get away from the awful scene, and soon were seated in the carriage, Minnie with her face buried in her perfumed handkerchief.

"O pa," she said, "why did you take me to such a place?"

"I urged you, child, not to enter."

"But I did not know what was there."

"You should have taken my advice."

"But I didn't know."

"Certainly you did not know. I would have saved your nerves this shock, but you persisted in going in."

"But, pa, why did *you* wish to go?"

"Because I came here to see all that was to be seen. I have often heard of the *Morgue*, and wished to see it. Now, if in future you will take my counsel in such cases, you will be saved some pain."

"O pa, do tell me whenever you are going to such a place again! Why, I tremble now."

"It was a sight, my child, enough to make one shudder."

"See! I believe it has struck Walter dumb."

They all looked to the lad, who, in one corner of the carriage, was sitting with a very grave look and a very sober face.

"What are you thinking about, Walter?" asked Mr. Tenant.

"I was thinking that any one of us might get separated from the rest, fall a victim to death, and be brought here, unrecognized and unknown."

"The thought is a natural one on leaving such a place. We should be careful and not be separated in this strange land."

"Yes; and we should remember," added Mr. Percy, "that the great and holy God watches over us here, as well as at home. The unseen hand of the heavenly Father holds and protects us. We are not the children of fate, nor chance, but the children of Providence."

"I remember that mother has often spoken to me of this Providence," said Walter.

"Did I not hear her repeating some lines to you the night before we left home?"

"Yes, sir."

"What were they? Can you repeat them?"

"I do not know — perhaps I can: —

>   'All nature is but art unknown to thee;
>   All chance, direction, which thou canst not see;
>   All discord ——'

I forget the other words."

Mr. Tenant added the rest: —

>   "—— harmony, not understood;
>   All partial evil, universal good."

"Who was the author of the lines, Walter?" asked his father.

"Pope; they are in his 'Essay on Man.' Mother was reading from that when you heard her."

Minnie, whose spirits were very elastic, soon recovered her cheerfulness; and, as the carriage passed through the gay streets of Paris, which were all alive with marching soldiers, gay women, and polite men, the whole company soon forgot the sad scene they had witnessed.

But as they rode along they were suddenly arrested; a crash occurred, a shout from the driver, and a roll of the carriage, which for the instant seemed to threaten the occupants with sudden disaster.

"Hold, driver, hold!" cried Mr. Percy, forgetting that the poor fellow could not understand him.

"Keep your arms from the doors, children," cried Mr. Tenant.

"O, dear, what is the matter?" asked Minnie.

"The matter is all over now," replied her father, as the carriage, relieved of its pressure, righted, and drove on.

"What was it, pa?"

"Why, did you not see? Our careless driver

got us wedged in between an omnibus and a dray."

"I wish the omnibus was driven from the streets. It is always in trouble."

"Foolish child, the omnibus is a very useful and economical conveyance."

"But how often they fill up Washington Street and Broadway, injuring lighter carriages!"

"Yet they are great conveniences. What would they do in London without them? You noticed how cheaply we could ride there in them."

"Well, I presume you are right; but I have often wondered why they call that long, ugly carriage, *omnibus*."

"Can Walter tell?" asked his father.

"Yes, sir; I recollect that our school teacher, Mr. Falkner, said it was a Latin word, that meant '*for all*,' or '*accommodate all*.'"

"How long have they been used, father?" asked the little girl.

"Well, a line was started here in 1828. The people of London established a line a year or two afterwards."

"Where did it run?"

"Through the Strand, I think."

"When did the Americans start them?"

"They claim to have had a line some years earlier."

"Where — in Boston?"

"No; in New York."

"Have they any horse railroads in London or Paris?"

"There are none in London, and only one in Paris; that runs from Paris to St. Cloud, and is called the American railway."

This conversation was interrupted by the sudden stoppage of the carriage.

"What is the matter now, driver?" asked Mr. Tenant.

The driver pointed to four dark-colored stones in the street, and seeing how earnest his gesticulations were, they concluded there was something to see.

"What is it?" they all asked.

The driver made them to understand that this was the place where the guillotine stands in case of public execution. Here, he told them, that fatal instrument was erected.

"Who was last executed here?"

"Orsini."

"Who was he, pa?" asked Minnie.

"He was an Italian, who endeavored to assassinate the emperor a short time ago."

"You told us, pa, that at some time convenient you would describe the guillotine — will you do so now?"

"If you wish to have me, I will."

"Why is it called guillotine?"

"From Joseph Ignatius Guillotin, a physician."

"Did he invent it?"

"No, not exactly. An instrument called the *maiden* was formerly used in England and Scotland for public executions, very similar to the guillotine. The Italians also had the *mannaia*, a similar machine. This physician, who died in 1814, proposed this mode of execution instead of hanging; and being adopted at his suggestion, the instrument took his name."

"What does the guillotine look like?"

"It somewhat resembles a pile-driver, which you have seen at work at home. There are two upright posts, with grooves. In these grooves runs a heavy iron knife. The criminal is laid between the posts, in a horizontal position, his face downward, directly beneath the knife, which is raised to a considerable height. At a given signal, a spring is touched, and the knife, or rather the iron weight with a sharpened edge, descends, and cuts off the head at once."

"How terrible!"

"And yet it was deemed a merciful change from hanging, or the English mode of decapitation with an axe."

"And this is the way in which the beautiful Marie Antoinette and her husband were executed?"

"Yes. I told you something about it when we were in the Place de la Concorde, and when we go out to Versailles, I shall have something more to say to you respecting these unfortunate people."

"O, how fearful!"

"Child, you can have no idea of it. Those scenes, never to be repeated, form one of the darkest days of France. It was awful to see that royal family perish so."

"Were they both executed together?"

"No; I think I told you the king was beheaded first. He was taken from prison, and carried to the place, and with a firm step ascended the platform, and — But it is a long story, which you must read."

"O, do go on!" cried both children at once.

"Well, the king stood on the platform. The plank, the rope, the knife, the pavements for yards around, were clotted with blood. Unresistingly he was bound to the plank, and the plank was placed beneath the axe which came gliding down, noiseless as lightning, and as fatal too; and the trunkless head of Louis XVI. rolled at the feet of the executioner.

"The queen lived a few months, in a cell, the floor of which was thick with mud and dust, the walls of which were covered with vermin, when she was taken out to hear her sentence — death. She ascended the steps; she trod on blood; she knelt in prayer, where it seemed as if God had forgotten to be merciful; she was bound to the plank; her eye watched for a moment the glittering knife; the plank was brought beneath the fatal groove; the axe fell, and the head of Maria Antoinette rolled into the basket, where it struck against the head of one of her noblest friends, who had gone to death before her."

"Here we are at Père la Chaise," said Mr. Tenant; "and a truce to these bloody stories, I say."

They all left the carriage and entered the gate, and were soon in this fairy place, admiring the beautiful monuments and tombs.

"What are all these little buildings for?" asked Minnie, pointing to chapels that decorate the place.

"They are built instead of monuments. There, go and look at that one that Walter seems to be admiring."

Minnie ran over to where Walter stood, with

his sketch book in his hand, taking a rough draft of one of the chapels.

"Let me see," she said, pulling his book.

The chapel which Walter had sketched was of soft sandstone, Corinthian architecture, seven feet long and four feet wide. A man could stand upright in it. The walls were thin, and the door of iron trellised work, through which the interior could be seen. It was furnished with a chair, a prayer book, several pots of the geranium, a vase of natural flowers, a kneeling statue, a silver crucifix, a miniature daguerreotype, a mourning picture, and some twenty-five wreaths of artificial flowers. A little table on which some of these things stood was covered with white muslin, and the floor neatly spread with painted carpet. In the rear, behind the altar, or table, was a small stained glass window; and the whole structure was neat and beautiful.

"How large is this cemetery?" asked Mr. Tenant of his friend.

"About one hundred acres, I believe."

"I do not think it so fine as Mount Auburn, or Greenwood," said Walter, who had finished his sketch.

"In some respects it is not," replied his father.

"Here, pa, what is this?" cried Minnie, pointing to a somewhat remarkable tomb.

"That is the famous tomb of Abelard and Héloïse."

"And who were they — monks, nuns, kings, or queens?"

"Perhaps Walter can tell you."

"Can you, Walter?"

"I have read something about them," replied the lad, "and if you will wait until we get home, I will tell you."

"I can't wait."

"Can't?"

"No. The story will be out of date then."

"Well, then, stop breaking that bush, and walk around the tomb with me, and I will tell you all I know."

"Go on; I am all attention."

"Abelard was a —"

"Was that all his name?"

"No. His name was Peter Abelard. He was a monk of St. Benedict, and a famous scholar. He was distinguished as a teacher and a man of science. In the city of Paris he met Héloïse."

"Who was she?"

"A young lady of great beauty, niece of a

distinguished personage. With her he fell in love, and —"

"Bah!"

"A secret marriage took place, which, to save her husband from the consequences, the lady denied under oath. Her friends proceeded to wreak vengeance on Abelard, and his prospects of usefulness and happiness were blasted. The monks pursued him with untiring ferocity for years, but he bore it all as a patient sufferer. He became Abbot of — of — Pa, can you tell me what Abelard was Abbot of?"

"Of St. Gildas de Rays," my son.

"Héloïse became the head of a religious sisterhood; and in connection with their sacred duties, they often saw each other. Abelard died at the age of sixty-three, venerated for his virtues. Héloïse begged his body, and at her death, which occurred soon after, was buried beside him. About sixty years ago their ashes were brought to this place and entombed."

"Well, well; why did Héloïse deny the marriage?"

"To shield Abelard."

"Why to shield him? What shield did he need?"

"He was an ecclesiastic, and according to the laws of the Romish church, could not marry."

"Ah."

"So it was, I believe."

"But how did you know so much about them?"

"Did you see me conversing with that old French *valet-de-place*, at the hotel, last night?"

"Yes."

"Well, he told me all I have told you."

"What else did he say?"

"He said that the affecting letters of Abelard and Héloïse had been published, and could not be read without tears."

"I will get them and read them."

"Walter," said Mr. Tenant, "here is a spot you will want to see."

"What, that bunch of weeds with a rough fence around it?"

"Yes."

"Who lies there?"

"Marshal Ney, whose only crime was that he loved his country too well, is here. After having fought the battles and avenged the wrongs of France, he was condemned and shot as a traitor; and his ashes are here, without a monument."

"I have read a sketch of him. He was a hero."

"Yes; but the fates of war decided his case.

He was shot to appease the allied powers, and now sleeps in a dishonored grave."

They wandered about a long time in the cemetery, and from the highest point obtained a fine view of the city in the distance. It seemed as if the children never would be tired, and long after the gentlemen were ready to return, Walter and Minnie sat on the brow of the hill, gazing off upon the gay, lively city, admiring what they saw, and begging permission to stay and enjoy the fine view, and the pleasant walks a little longer.

Chapter V.

GLIMPSES AT FRENCH ROYALTY.

THE French people have often changed their form of government, and sometimes have had no government at all. Now it is king, and then emperor, and anon president. To-day it is Bourbon, and to-morrow Orleans. The fickle French, in their love of change, do not make the throne an easy seat; but under their restless desires for something new, the Tuileries often change occupants.

"I have seen the emperor," cried Walter, running into his father's room one evening, as the gentlemen of the party sat conversing together.

"Where, Walter?" asked Minnie, starting up from the bed in her own little apartment, upon which she had thrown herself.

"He was on horseback, and returning from some excursion, escorted by some mounted soldiers."

"How did he look?"

"Like any other man, I believe. I only had a glimpse as he rode by."

"Shall we see the emperor and empress?" he asked, turning to his father.

"I think we shall."

"How?"

"O, I have means of obtaining a sight of these illustrious persons, that you will find out soon."

"I would like to know something about the French government before I see the emperor," said Minnie.

"What would you like to know, my child?"

"Well, about the kings and queens."

"That history is long and full. This country has had many noted sovereigns. The illustrious Charlemagne once ruled here, and —"

"Who was he?"

"He was one of the earlier sovereigns, under whose reign France increased in power, literary culture, and social importance. He was born in 742, was crowned king of the Franks at the age of twenty-six; and after many brilliant exploits, died in 814."

"Was he buried in Paris?"

"No; in Aix-la-Chapelle, a place you will visit while we are on the continent, when I will give you some further particulars of this king."

"I have heard, father," said Walter, "that Charlemagne was buried in a sitting posture."

"Yes; he was seated on a throne of gold; his crown was put on his head, his sceptre in his hand; by his side were his shield and sword, and on his knees were the Gospels according to the four evangelists. An arch of triumph was erected over the vault, and on it an inscription placed."

"What was it?"

"As near as I remember, it was in these words: 'Here lies the body of Charles, the great and orthodox Emperor, who gloriously enlarged, and for forty-seven years happily governed, the Empire of the Franks.'"

"I have read, pa, the history of France, down to the revolution, and I have often wondered why the people should drive away so good a king as Louis Philippe."

"There were many reasons for it, my son. Louis Philippe came to the throne in 1830, in the midst of the existence of several distinct parties. The republicans were clamorous for a democracy; the legitimists for the restoration of the elder branch of the Bourbon family; while a middle class looked to the house of Orleans as the only hope of their blood-drunken nation. Lafayette presented Louis Philippe as the representative of a liberal government; and he was accepted by the people, and crowned accordingly. But he was not a warlike man, and failed to satisfy the thirst of the people for military glory."

"Was his reign, while it lasted, peaceful?"

"Not for him. From the day of his coronation up to the year 1848, he continued to reign, his throne ever surrounded by traitors, frequent attempts made upon his life, and storm and tempest continually howling around him. The poor man did not have much comfort on his throne."

"He was a good king — was he not?"

"Yes, he was, on the whole, a good king, a man of tolerable intellect, with a good knowledge of human nature, and an instinctive love of peace and order. During his administration, public buildings were erected, the arts flourished, and the nation was prosperous and happy. But, overlooking all these considerations, the people thirsted for revolution."

"Why could he not have crushed out this revolution? He had soldiers enough."

"He might have done it. While the bells were tolling, and the people were gathering in the street, the Tuileries was filled with counsellors, M. Molé, M. Thiers, M. Guizot, and others having been called in to consult with the perplexed king. These all advised immediate and decided action; but the peaceful king was unwilling to shed blood, and hesitated. The commandant told him that the revolution could be stayed; that one broadside would drive back the masses who were filling the Place de la Concorde. Still the king wished to avoid the slaughter, and refused the counsel. At last the monarch gave orders to have the soldiers fire upon the mob. But the officer shook his head, and exclaimed, ' *Too late !* ' "

" What did the king do then ? "

" He abdicated."

" What is that ? " asked Minnie.

" A resignation of the kingly office. Louis Philippe abdicated in favor of the Count of Paris."

" Who was he ? "

" He was grandson of the king, the oldest son of the Duke of Orleans."

" Did he become king ? "

" No ; his mother, the Duchess of Orleans, went to the Chamber of Deputies, with her two children, and pleaded for their rights, while over her hung the sword, and around her shouted the infuriated madmen. She was a widow, and arrayed in mourning for the sad death of her husband, who was thrown from his carriage and killed a while before, about which sad accident I will tell you at some future time."

"What did the deputies do?"

"At first they were touched with her appeal, and seemed about to acknowledge the young count as king; but a crowd of assailants burst into the chamber, and looked with glaring eyes upon the beautiful duchess and her children, and began to cry, 'Why is she here?' The tide which was setting towards royalty began to roll back again, and the defenceless woman was soon obliged to flee for her life. A butcher's boy, with a long knife in his hand, ran towards the duchess, crying, 'The spawn of royalty — we must make an end of them.'"

"Did he strike her?"

"No; he was held back by a brave son of old Marshal Soult, who hurled him down into the crowd with just indignation and abhorrence."

"And then?"

"She was forced out of the hall, and left in the crowd without. Here she was separated from her children, and, covered with a veil which concealed her countenance, she was dashed about by the swarms of people, until she fell against a glass door, which yielded, and she was borne away to a place of safety."

"What became of the young count?"

"He was recognized, and a brawny man was about strangling him in the streets, when he was rescued by a national guard, who carried him, at the risk of his own life, to his mother."

"You say there were two children?"

"Yes."

"What was the name of the other? Who was he?"

"The young Duke of Chartres."

"What became of him?"

"He fell in the street, and was trodden down by the mob. Rescued at length, he was taken away, and for several days his mother remained, without any knowledge of his safety, in the most distressing anxiety."

"Where were the rest of the family all this time?"

"The king, with the queen and their children, had fled as far as Dreux, where he heard that his abdication had not saved the throne to his grandson. He now began to fear for his own safety. The sad fate of Louis XVI. was before his mind, and he resolved to escape at once to England. Under the name of Theodore Lebran, he succeeded in the attempt, while his youngest son, the Duke of Montpensier, with his wife fled to Brussels."

"Did they all get to England?"

"Yes."

"Is the Count of Paris now alive?"

"Yes; and some think he will yet be king."

"When did Louis Napoleon appear?"

"Very soon after these events transpired."

"Father, will you tell me something about his early life?"

"It is a very curious history."

"That is why we want to hear it."

"The present emperor, Charles Louis Napoleon, is the son of Louis Bonaparte, ex-king of Holland."

"Who was he?"

"He was Napoleon's brother, the fourth son of Charles Bonaparte. When his brother became emperor, he was made king of Holland."

"Who was the present emperor's mother?"

"She was Hortensia Beauharnais, the step-daughter of Napoleon. Thus the present monarch is nephew of the great emperor, and grandson of Josephine."

"Yes, I understand."

"The marriage between Louis and Hortensia was forced on by Napoleon against the wishes of the parties most interested, but they found it impossible to resist the pressure. Louis himself, describing the marriage, says, "Never was there a more gloomy ceremony; never had husband and wife a stronger presentiment of the bitterness of a reluctant and ill-assorted union."

"And the present emperor was their son?"

"Yes; but the world heard little of him, though he was created Grand Duke of Berg, and was a great favorite with the old emperor."

"What next?"

"He first presented himself to the world in an insurrection at Strasburg, which was badly planned, and resulted most unfavorably. The garrison, consisting of several regiments, and the people, were enthusiastic in his favor. But owing to the most unskilful generalship, he lost his cause. Scarcely a blow was struck, or a gun fired, or a drop of blood shed. A stern royalist ran in among his own soldiers, and declared to them that the person calling himself Louis Napoleon, nephew of the emperor, was only an impostor. They became clamorous at once, and demanded that Louis Napoleon should prove his identity; and before he could do this, his camp was in complete disorder, and he was taken prisoner.

"Louis Napoleon thus describes the scene: 'A single word from myself, or Colonel Taillandier, would have led to a regular massacre. The officers around me repeatedly offered to hew me a passage through the infantry, which could have been easily effected; but I would not consent to shed French blood in my own cause; besides, I could not believe that the 46th regiment, which a moment previously had manifested so much sympathy, could have so promptly changed their sentiments. At any risk I determined to make an effort to recover my influence over it, and I suddenly rushed into their very midst; but in a minute I was surrounded by a triple row of bayonets, and forced to draw my sabre to parry off the blows aimed at me from every side. In another instant I should have perished by French hands, when the cannoneers, perceiving my danger, charged, and carrying me off, placed me in their ranks. Unfortunately, this movement separated me from my officers, and threw me amongst soldiers who doubted my identity. Another struggle ensued, and in a few minutes I was a prisoner.'"

"Did he originate this insurrection in order to overturn the king and get the throne?"

"Yes; but it proved a miserable failure."

"And then?"

"He instigated an insurrection at Boulogne, which was as badly managed, and resulted as disgracefully as the other; and he was shut up by the French government in the citadel of Ham, where he remained until he was made president, which office he held, you know, before he was made emperor."

"Have you ever seen the emperor, pa?"

"Yes, I have seen him once."

"How does he look?"

"Well, you will see him before you leave France, so that you can judge for yourself."

"His life is a strange one."

"Very. He was once a poor fellow in New York, wandering about living by his wits. He was also at one time a menial in the employ of the London police department."

"Were you ever at Hoboken, Minnie?" asked Mr. Tenant.

"No, sir," replied the little girl. "What of Hoboken? I know where it is."

"In that place is a small, mean hotel, built of wood, that is called 'Hotel Napoleon.' There at that hotel, now kept by a Frenchman, Louis Napoleon lived when he was in America. When you visit your friends in New York again, ask them to take you over and see it."

"I will, certainly; but was he poor at that time?"

"His means were quite limited, and it has been hinted that he could not pay his bill when he left."

"Ha, ha! that is good for an emperor!"

"But, father," asked Walter, "how did Louis Napoleon become emperor? You said he was made president."

"He was president for some years, until all became convinced that a republic could not exist in France. Indeed it was a republic only in name. The press was proscribed, the people crushed, and the whole nation was dissatisfied. At length, the famous *coup d'état* put an end to the republic, and —"

"Coo-de-tah! What does that mean?" asked Minnie.

"Why, it means," replied Mr. Percy, "a masterly stroke of policy, which I will explain. Napoleon found that the officers of his army were plotting against him — that the republican leaders were bent on his overthrow. So by one grand blow he determined to consummate his ambitious schemes. On the night of the first of December, 1851, a public reception was given by the president, which was attended by the most distinguished men of the chamber of deputies, and of the army. It was the day before the blow was to be struck against Napoleon, and late at night the lamps were extinguished, and the foes of Napoleon departed to dream of success the next day. They had all been deceived by the bland manner of the president. But no sooner were they gone, than he issued an order for their arrest; and before morning, every one of them was imprisoned."

"Were they not brave men?"

"Yes, of course."

"Why did they allow themselves to be arrested?"

"They were taken at a disadvantage, and resistance would have been useless. Some of them did make a show of opposition. General Changarnier, as the officials entered, snatched up a brace of pistols, and exclaimed, 'I am armed.' The officer told him it was of no use to resist, and he soon surrendered."

"What others?"

"Colonel Charras, being captured in bed, refused to get up, refused to dress himself, and declared that they should take him as he was, if they took him at all."

"Did they?"

"Yes; they bundled him up in some blankets, and thus conveyed him to prison."

"Were there any others?"

"Several; and among them General Cavaignac, who was soon to be married to a Mademoiselle Odier. He dressed himself very politely, and went to the prison."

"How did the lady — Mademoiselle — what did you call her — feel about it?"

"She acted like a true lady. Cavaignac at once wrote to her as follows: 'You have youth, beauty, accomplishments, wealth; a throng of admirers, young, and more meritorious than I am, surround you. Choose from among them, and you will be nearly as happy as you deserve to be — happier than I can make you.'"

"What did the lady reply?"

"That her love for him was changeless."

"Were they ever married?"

"Yes; when the general was liberated, he and the lady went to the Archbishop of Paris to be married. The bride was a Protestant, and the ecclesiastic would not perform the service unless she would promise to have the children educated in the Catholic faith. She refused, and they went to Holland and were married there."

"But, father," said Minnie, "you have not told us any thing about the empress. I am more interested in her."

"I have wondered that you have not asked about her before."

"Who is she?"

"She is a descendant of an ancient Scotch family, tracing her ancestry back to Sir Roger Kirkpatrick, who was intimately associated with

Robert Bruce. A descendant of Sir Roger, settled in Spain, married a daughter of Baron Grivegnée, of Malaga. By this marriage he had three children, one of whom was married to Count de Téba, who afterwards inherited the title of Count Montijo. The youngest daughter of the Count and Countess de Montijo is now empress of the French nation, Eugenie Countess de Téba."

"How did the emperor become acquainted with her?"

"She was educated at the convent of Sacre Cœur, in Paris, and thus fell in the way of the emperor."

"I would like to know how she looks."

"I can tell you," said Mr. Tenant.

"Can you? If so, you shall have my thanks."

"I saw to-day, in a London paper, a description of her person," said Mr. Tenant, turning over the newspapers on his table. "Ah, here it is; read it, Walter."

Walter took the paper and read. "The empress is about thirty years of age; she possesses considerable personal attractions, but more in the style of English than of Spanish beauty. Her complexion is transparently fair, her features regular, yet full of expression. She is of middle stature, or a little above it, with, as no doubt Louis Napoleon has found to be the case, manners extremely winning; her education is superior to that received generally by Spanish women who do not travel, and she is said to be what the Spaniards term *graciosa*, the French *spirituelle*. Her paternal fortune is, without being considerable, yet suitable to the rank her family holds in Spain — that of grandees of the first class. Her mother, the Countess of Montijo, has been for years at the head of the *haut ton* of Madrid, and her house has on more than one occasion been honored by the presence of royalty; and those who are acquainted with Spanish manners well know such an honor, from its rare occurrence, is most appreciated in Spain. Formerly it was the custom to suspend a chain across the doorway of the house the king had visited, and the haughtiest hidalgo of Castile pointed to that most expressive symbol of devotedness with pride. The receptions of the Countess de Montijo at Madrid comprised all that was most select and distinguished in rank and eminence in Spanish society."

"This is not very definite. What queen is she most like, Mr. Tenant?" asked Minnie.

"She is said to resemble Josephine more than any other royal personage."

THE PRESENTATION.

"Come, children," said Mr. Percy, "it is time you were both in bed."

"What o'clock is it, father?"

"Nearly ten."

Soon both children were in profound slumber, — kings, queens, and emperors being forgotten.

The next morning the whole party visited the Tuileries. Just as they were entering the yard, the emperor drove out with a mounted escort. The children both waved their handkerchiefs, and the monarch, observing it, saluted them in token of recognition, which pleased them very much. As they advanced, they saw a group of ladies on the Grand Stairs, and Mr. Percy whispered, "The empress!" And so it was — Eugenie in company with the Queen of Holland and the ladies of the court. The gentlemen passed on, of course, but the children lingered, which the empress observing, kindly addressed them, and seemed quite interested when they told her they were Americans. She also pointed to the prince imperial, who was amusing himself with his nurse at a little distance. Then they ran after the gentlemen, who were waiting for them, Minnie exclaiming, —

"How beautiful she looks!"

Walter was as enthusiastic in his expressions of admiration, and both coincided with the gentlemen who thought the kindly recognition of the empress a very gracious act of courtesy. All day the children were talking about the empress, and their older friends were almost wearied with it. After this, they often saw the royal family riding out, though the emperor was seldom with the empress. Before they left the city, they also had the honor of a presentation to the royal family. In company with several others, some of whom were military officers, they paid their respects to the royal family, and saw the young prince imperial, who was born March 16, 1856, and who is an object of much interest to the French people.

Chapter VI.

PARIS BY SUN LIGHT AND GAS LIGHT.

IT would take a long time to tell all the places visited by our party, for there are few cities in the world that have so many objects of interest, and so many attractive features. The children expected much pleasure, and so were pleased with almost every thing they saw. Sometimes, when they felt a little homesick, and failed to receive a letter from mother, or any of the friends at home, they would say, that to them Paris was not half so beautiful as Boston, and that they would give more for Boston Common than for all the pleasure grounds of France; but those feelings would soon be lost in delight at the beautiful scenes and charming prospects that every where presented themselves.

One evening, Mr. Percy said to them, "Now we have been in Paris two weeks, and have seen many things of interest, and there remain many more to be seen. I propose that we be as systematic as possible in seeing what remain.

Walter, what have you on your list, that we must visit?"

"Several places we have not seen yet, and some we have seen we must go to again."

"Read your list down."

"He probably has a whole list of tombs, or ruins, or catacombs, or something."

"Certainly, I have something, Min. Let me read.

"The Invalides, the —"

"Invalids? What, hospital patients?"

"Hush, Minnie! The Gobelins, the —"

"What Goblins — turkeys?"

"Be still, and let me read."

"Minnie," said Mr. Percy, "be quiet while Walter reads. Your conduct annoys us as well as him."

Walter read over a long list, and it was concluded to go out and see the various objects as soon as possible. So the next morning they started. They gave the driver of the carriage the names of the places to which they wanted to go, and he, taking the most distant first, drove out to the *abattoirs* of Montmartre.

"What are the *abattoirs*?" asked Minnie, as they rode along.

"They are immense places for the slaughter of animals. We wish to go in and see them;

but we will leave you in the carriage, if you wish."

"I wish to see, though the sight may not be a very pleasant one."

"You had better not go in; it is not a very proper place for a little lady like you."

"Why, pa, I can stand any thing."

"Remember the Morgue, my child."

"Ough!"

"I am glad we are going there," said Walter, "for ever since I have been here, I have desired to know how these thousands of people are fed."

"It is a matter of some wonder, I admit. I have seen it stated that last year there were consumed sixty-two million pounds of meat of the various kinds."

"Whew!"

"There were also drank here, last year, three million two hundred thousand gallons of wine, one hundred and seventy-seven thousand gallons of alcohol, forty-five thousand gallons of cider."

"What drinkers!"

"There was also eaten four hundred thousand dollars' worth of oysters, one million seven hundred and fifty thousand dollars' worth of fish, fresh and salt, three million five hundred and fifty thousand dollars' worth of poultry, and three million seven hundred and eighty thousand dollars' worth of butter, besides many other things."

"Well, pa, how does the consumption agree with the use of the same articles in New York and other American cities?"

"I have not statistics at hand to tell, but have seen it stated that there were consumed the same year in New York one hundred and fifty million pounds of beef alone, against sixty-two million pounds of all kinds of meat in Paris."

"What is the difference in the population of the two cities?"

"Paris has one million five hundred thousand inhabitants, and New York has less than a million."

They had now arrived at the *abattoirs*, and Minnie remained in the carriage while the gentlemen and Walter went in. They were pleased with the skill with which the cattle were killed and prepared for market, and with the extent of these sources of public sustenance; and Mr. Tenant, as they returned to the carriage, declared that no person interested in sanitary matters of a city should neglect visiting these *abattoirs* when in Paris.

They then drove to a very different place — the Hotel Royal des Invalides, or royal home for invalid soldiers, where there are several thousands of old soldiers, with some of whom the children conversed, they being able to speak English. As they entered, they found a company of Napoleon's old soldiers drawn up for review. Some had legs, and some had eyes; but the majority of them were in some way disabled.

"Who are these?" asked Minnie.

Her father told her; whereupon she was much interested, and asked, "Did they fight beneath Napoleon's eye?"

"Yes; and it is an affecting sight to see these old soldiers, whose faces will now kindle up with enthusiasm at the mention of Waterloo, Austerlitz, and Lodi."

"Who is that, pa?" cried the child, pointing to an elderly officer who was advancing.

"It is Napoleon I. himself," cried Walter, turning in the direction in which his sister was pointing.

"Hush, children!" said Mr. Percy; "that is Jerome Bonaparte, Napoleon's brother, the Ex-King of Westphalia."

As he approached, he courteously saluted the party, recognizing them as strangers. Walter was much pleased, and could hardly believe that he was not in the presence of the great emperor himself, so much does Jerome look like the pictures of his illustrious relative.

They all then began to look about the noble edifice. It was originally a magnificent church, and several buildings have been added to it, forming a grand hospital for disabled soldiers. In the centre beneath the dome is the tomb which is being prepared for the remains of Napoleon. This tomb is a circular apartment sunk in the floor, forming a crypt which is open to the view from above, and a marble balustrade allows the spectator to go and look down upon the spot where the hero is to lie. This spacious and elegant gallery beneath the ground is worthy of the hero's fame. Statues, monuments, beautiful bass-reliefs, all vie with each other to add beauty to the sepulchre of imperial greatness. The coffin into which the body is to be put is of porphyry, a single block twelve feet long and six wide. The remains are not yet placed in this receptacle, but are in one of the chapels on the side of the building. There the conqueror lies in a black ebony coffin, his old hat that you see in all the pictures, and the sword he wore at Austerlitz, are lying on the coffin. Several stands of bullet-riddled, faded, blood-stained colors hang over the coffin, and these are all that remain of that mighty man! this is the end of the conqueror!

The party wandered about the structure, entering the tombs of Duroc and Bertrand, gazing on the grand altar, or looking through elegant iron and bronze railing that separates the dome from the church, and admiring all they saw.

"Why were Duroc and Bertrand thus honored in being allowed a resting-place in such pomp here?" asked Walter.

"On account of their distinguished services to the emperor."

"Who were they, pa?" asked Minnie.

"Duroc was a grand marshal, a strong friend of the emperor, and was killed at Bautzen, in 1813. While he was dying, he was visited by Napoleon, to whom he said, 'My whole life has been devoted to you, and I only regret that I am about to lose it, because it might still be of service to you.' 'Duroc,' replied Napoleon, 'there is another world after this, and there it is that we shall one day meet again.' Duroc and Napoleon have met."

"Who was Bertrand?"

"Why, Minnie, have you never heard of him? Walter can tell you about him, I know."

"Can you, Walter?"

"Yes; he also was a grand marshal, as well as aid-de-camp to the emperor."

"What is an aid-de-camp?"

"He is one who receives from a general the orders, and transmits them to others."

"Yes, I see."

"Bertrand followed Napoleon to Elba, and also to St. Helena, and was with him in his dying struggles, and closed his eyes when he was dead."

They spent some time at the Invalides, and then rode to the armory, or Artillery Museum, where they saw an immense number of models of all sorts of military articles, from a rifle to a huge fortification; the real weapons, some old and rusty, dug up from battle fields, and some inlaid with gems, the gift of kings, and all the military ensigns usually found in such a place. Walter, as they left, declared that the Museum looked very much more like real, practical warfare, than the armory in London Tower. With the remark the gentlemen coincided.

"One place more let us go to to-day," said Walter, as they left the armory.

"Where, my son?" asked his father.

"Hotel de Cluny."

"Well."

"I wonder what kind of a place that can be?" said Minnie, half to herself, and half aloud.

"You will see, sis."

So they drove on until they came to Cluny, once the residence of the abbots of that name, where they found a great many antiquities, which pleased Walter very much; but which Minnie declared were not worth looking at. They also went into some old Roman ruins near by, called Palais des Thermes, formerly the residence of several Roman emperors. They could all see that it must once have been a very stately and imposing edifice. Julian resided there when he was proclaimed emperor.

This visit ended the day's work, and they were all glad to get to the hotel; and after a late dinner, the children wrote a while, and then retired early to rest, the gentlemen going out to see Paris by gas light.

"Where are we going now?" said Minnie to her father, the next morning, as they rode out.

"To the Gobelins."

"What are they?"

"An immense tapestry manufactory, where the most exquisite articles of that kind are made."

"But why call such an establishment 'The Gobelins'?"

"The establishment is named for one Jean

Gobelin, who commenced the business some four or five centuries ago. He was succeeded by several other private persons, and the whole establishment at length fell into the hands of the government; and one hundred and twenty hands are now employed in the manufacture of the most beautiful fabrics for the state."

When they reached the place, they were admitted at once, and taken first into the exhibition rooms, where they saw several very rich pieces, softer and more exquisite than painting. The children gazed on them for some time, and the excellence of several they detected and pointed out. One especially seemed to draw the attention of Minnie. It was a scene from the history of Napoleon. He had arrived at the sad conclusion of obtaining a divorce from his beautiful Empress Josephine. Actuated by political motives, and impelled by an uncontrollable ambition, he had already taken the steps necessary in such a case. A letter is sent from one of Napoleon's marshals, announcing to the wife the plans of the emperor. This tapestry represents Josephine laying the letter before her husband, and appealing to him to deny its contents. The whole scene is one of touching beauty. Josephine is on her knees; the tears are rolling down her cheeks; the open letter is in her jewelled hands; while her whole countenance bears the marks of the most beautiful grief and anxiety. Napoleon stands before her, with scarcely less of sorrow on his own countenance; and he turns half away, to hide his feelings. Without the door are listening figures, ready to catch the words uttered, and go away and spread them through the metropolis. The figures are as large as life, and wrought in a most perfect manner.

"Did Josephine love Napoleon, Mr. Tenant?" asked Minnie of that gentleman.

"Yes, dear. She loved him with undying and untiring affection; his battles she watched with the most painful interest; and in all France there was not a truer heart than hers even after the sad divorce."

"They were unlike."

"Yes. She was lovely, gentle, and dove-like; he was fiery, impetuous, and strong. She clung to him as the vine clings to the mighty oak."

"Did he love her?"

"Yes, very much."

"Why, then, did he divorce her?"

"For political reasons, which at some other time I will explain to you."

They saw a great many pieces of this work, and then went into the rooms where it was being manufactured. They saw the slow and tedious process, and wondered how the men could have patience to work on so. They saw there portraits, most exquisitely wrought, of the emperor and empress. As Minnie saw the latter, she cried, —

"Hold me up, Mr. Tenant."

"Where? how? what?"

"Why, to the empress's face; I want to kiss her, she looks so life-like."

Mr. Tenant held her up, and she kissed the silent but life-like lips, while Walter stood laughing at her.

They then rode to the Jardin des Plantes, a famous place, on which Buffon, the naturalist, has expended so much of his genius. This garden was laid out by Louis XIII., and has become a favorite resort. Here the children saw an extensive menagerie, a collection of natural history, all kinds of plants, and a great many very interesting things. They wandered about so much here, that at the close of the visit they did not want to go any where else. They were very tired, though neither of them was willing to confess it.

On the way home, they drove through the Place de la Bastille, where a commemorative pillar now stands. As they rode along, Mr. Percy gave the

SCENE ON THE BOULEVARDS.

children a brief sketch of the old Bastille, of the enormities once committed within its walls, of the events of that dreadful day when the enraged populace took it and destroyed it, and sent, as a memorial, a stone from its walls to every town in France. While the children sat in the carriage the gentlemen went to the top of the pillar, from whence they had a fine view of Paris. When they came down, they told Walter that the gallery at the summit was all covered over with a wire netting, so that no person could cast himself off, and that the gallery is up two hundred and ten steps from the ground.

As the children were waiting for the gentlemen, they were much amused at a man with a sort of exhibition, who, as he saw them waiting, came very near and began to show his automaton figures, a view of which is on the preceding page.

One day in Paris was spent in seeing the churches, many of which are very interesting specimens of architecture, and not a few of which have peculiar and thrilling historical reminiscences connected with them. The children looked with wonder on the vast outlines and noble proportions of Notre Dame, which stands on the site of an ancient Roman temple, and is nearly ten centuries old. Two towers surmount the structure, from which a fine view of Paris is obtained, in one of which is an enormous bell, weighing thirty-two thousand pounds, that sends out its iron tone like the voice of a giant. A guide went in with our friends, and as he took them about he said to Minnie, —

"See here!"

"What now?"

"You are standing on the very spot where Napoleon was married to Josephine."

"Ah!"

"Yes; and I will show you the robes worn by the pope when he married them."

"What pope?"

"Pius VII."

"What are these bones?" asked Walter, a moment after, as they saw in a side chapel two small bones of the back, and between them a bullet.

"They are bones from the body of the archbishop, who was killed in a late revolution."

"What, was he a fighting man?"

"No. He was an amiable man, and his fall was much lamented. When blood was flowing in the streets of Paris, he went out, regardless of his own safety, to stay the crimson tide. Wherever he was recognized his authority was respected, and he moved from street to street, quelling the fury of the misguided populace. But at length, while climbing over a barricade in one of the streets, a random shot was fired, which killed him."

"And what does that group of statuary represent?" said Minnie, pointing to a piece over a tomb.

"That statuary," said the guide, "is of extraordinary origin. The wife of an Austrian nobleman had a singular dream. She saw her husband in a coffin, and engaged in a fearful struggle with embodied death. He called for her to help him; but she was powerless, and the monster performed his work. She awoke, and her dream was over; but in a few days she learned that, at the very hour of her sleep, her husband was accidentally killed. She had a group of statuary made to represent her dream; and here it stands, to remind every beholder of his own conflict with the powers of death."

They saw many other things which interested them very much; and when they went out they saw several men, with long brushes, well wet with holy water, to touch those who might desire the application. They also went to St. Germain l'Auxerrois, founded by Childeric, in 580, and which has been sacked and rebuilt several times since;—it was the bell on this church that sounded the signal for the commencement of the massacre of St. Bartholomew's day;—to St. Eustache, one of the most beautiful in Paris, and in the vaults of which many eminent personages are buried; to St. Roch, the richest parish in the city, which is distinguished for many revolutionary scenes, and to many others of interest to the stranger.

" Let us go to the palaces to-day," said Minnie one morning, just as they were starting out.

" What palaces ? " asked her father.

" All of them."

" Well, if that is agreeable to the rest of the company, we will."

In accordance with this, they directed their steps to the Tuileries, the residence of the French monarchs, and for an hour revelled in the halls of kings. The children were delighted with the elegance of the apartments, the gold and silver hangings, the silk and damask drapery, the immense chandeliers that light as the sun these halls at night, and make one feel, as he walks through the palace, like one in an enchanted castle. But the memories of the past are grander than these ancient halls themselves. Here Napoleon and Josephine — that greatest of heroes, that most amiable but most unfortunate of wives — lived and walked. In this chamber they slept; in that they formed together those plans which made the name of Bonaparte famous in all lands. Here, when the empire was overthrown, and the republic of an hour was stranded, lived Louis Philippe. Here on that fatal day when anarchy surged around his throne, and innumerable voices were shouting for his blood, met Thiers, Barrot, Emile de Girardin, and a company of true men, to consult with the perplexed and agitated king; and it was from these halls that one of the best of kings, the father of his people, went forth, repeating as he crossed the Place de la Concorde, "*Une grande infortune!*" Then the palace was turned into barracks; coarse, rough citizens thronged the sleeping and dressing rooms of the queens and empresses; and for ten days the filthy herd revelled in their beastliness beneath columns which had echoed with the merriment of nobles and kings. The present emperor now resides in this palace. The private apartments of Louis Philippe are used as the bed chamber and dressing rooms of the empress, and in her absence are shown to strangers. They are the same rooms which once were occupied by Marie Antoinette, and are consecrated by several affecting scenes in the life of that gifted but unfortunate woman.

Then they went to the Louvre, near by, where they walked through the various halls and galleries, some silent and deserted, some gorgeous with splendor and life-like with pictures.

"What room is this?" asked Walter, as they entered a most magnificent apartment, in which were crowds of admiring people.

"This is the famous Apollo Gallery," replied his father.

"Famous for what?"

"Why, among other things, for its size — one hundred and eighty feet in length, and twenty-eight in breadth; and lighted, as you see, by twenty-one great windows. You also see how beautiful the ceiling is."

"Then, Walter," said Mr. Tenant, "there are many historical reminiscences connected with this room. It is associated with the old Bourbon monarchs, with Louis Philippe, with Napoleon, with Marie Antoinette, with Josephine, and with the present emperor and empress. It was in this room that the empire was given to Louis Napoleon by the French senate."

They admired it very much, and then passed into other galleries, but lingered longest among the works of art which they found. Minnie made the acquaintance of a lady artist, who, in the immense picture gallery, was painting from one of the old pictures, and found her to be an English girl, who was passionately fond of this art.

They stood in the balcony where, it is said, Charles IX. stood and fired at Protestants, at the massacre of St. Bartholomew's day, which the young reader would do well to read about in some reliable historical work.

From the Louvre they went to the Palace of Luxembourg, built by Mary de' Medici, a structure finished in the most elaborate and elegant style, where there were galleries of paintings, halls of sculpture, and schools of art. About a year after the Percy family visited the palace, a fire broke out, and various parts of the edifice were consumed — the beautiful senate house, with its dome of glass, fell in.

As they stood looking upon the finished walls and elegant ceiling of this palace, Minnie remarked, —

"Walter, Harry St. Clair would not believe you, if you should give him a description of this magnificent place."

"Why not, sis?"

"I know he would not."

"What makes you think so?"

"Because the day before we left home, I met him in the street, and told him what beautiful buildings we expected to see abroad, and he said that we should not see any such elegant buildings as we thought we should; and he also told me that the Music Hall was more elegant than any building in the old world."

"Ha, ha, ha!"

"He said a Mr. Somebody told him so."

"Ha, ha, ha! that is good for Harry St. Clair!"

One day, when the party were riding out, they came to the Chapel of St. Ferdinand, a little church-like looking structure, into which they entered.

"I believe, children, I promised to tell you something about the Duke of Orleans, father of the Count of Paris — did I not?"

"Yes, yes, you did, pa!" said Minnie.

"O, yes, you so promised," said Walter.

"Well, I will now redeem the promise."

"We should be glad to hear how he died."

"The story is one of much interest. He was out, riding in his carriage, when the horses became unmanageable; and, in endeavoring to leap to the ground, his foot was entangled, and, being precipitated to the earth, his skull was fractured. He was taken up and carried into a grocery on the spot where the chapel now stands."

"Did he die alone?"

"No; his father, Louis Philippe, and the other members of the royal family, were soon on the ground; but the unfortunate young man died in a few hours after."

"In a grocery, did you say?"

"Yes; and afterwards the grocery was taken down, and a chapel, dedicated to St. Ferdinand, was erected on the spot."

They looked about the chapel, which has seats for about fifty persons, and is fifty feet long, built in Gothic style. Opposite the doorway is the altar, and over it a statue of the Virgin and Child. On the left side of the chapel is another altar. On the right is a beautiful group of statuary, representing the prince on his death bed, with an angel kneeling over him. This angel was the work of the Princess Marie, the deceased sister of the duke, who little dreamed that she was fashioning the marble for the monumental tomb of her brother. Behind the altar is the little room in which the prince died, remaining nearly as at that time. A few rough chairs, a confessional and crucifix, constitute the only furniture. On one side is a mournful picture representing the death scene as it actually occurred. The **duke is** stretched upon **a** bed, **pale and bleeding.** The king holds his hands, with a countenance full of the deepest grief; the queen and many of the nobles are looking on, weeping in the most abject sorrow; while a robed priest, with a benign countenance, adds to the effect of the scene.

There was also another chapel visited by the children, which interested them very much — the Chapelle Expiatoire.

"What is this, pa?" asked Minnie.

"I will tell you. When the revolution had beheaded Louis XVI. and **Marie Antoinette,** they **were put** into coarse coffins, **and** buried in a little cemetery belonging to the church of La Madeleine. On the records of that church is now a charge like this: '*For the coffin of the widow Capet, seven francs;*' **and this was the whole sum** laid out for the interment of the gifted, beautiful, and high-born queen, **whose** word once made nobles tremble."

"O, how **sad!**"

"**The** ground was afterwards purchased by **a** stern royalist, who planted it as an orchard, that the traces of the graves might not lead to a discovery, fearing that, in some wild **and** terrible moment, the populace might dig **up the bones,** and insult even their decay."

"Would they have done that?"

"They might, and he wished to guard against it. When monarchy was restored, the ground was purchased by the government, and a neat chapel erected over the spot where the king and queen were interred."

"What an interesting spot!"

"Yes; and let me tell you, children, something about a person whom I met in this chapel some years ago."

"Who was it?" asked the two children in one breath."

"The Duchess of Angoulême, who, within a few years, has been called from earth. She was the daughter of Louis XVI. and Marie Antoinette."

"Do tell us about her."

"I do not know much except the general facts. At the time of the murder, she was but a child, and, with her brother, the dauphin, about whom I have told you, then only seven years old, was shut up in a dark and gloomy dungeon. The boy was soon let out to a brutal keeper, who had orders not to kill him, but to *get rid of him*. Hence every indignity was heaped upon him. For a whole year his clothes were not changed; and for six months his bed was not made. Under such treatment the young dauphin died in June, 1795. His sister was at length allowed to go to Austria, and she lived until a few years since."

There were a great many places visited by the party while they were in Paris; and among others, Hotel de Ville, the magnificent town hall, or city hall, the Palace of Industry, the building erected for the world's exhibition in the Champs Elysees, the Royal Library, several public gardens, and many other places and objects, all of which Walter wrote down a description of in his journal, that by this time had become a very portentous volume.

Chapter VII.

THREE WAYS FOR SUNDAY.

A PERSON accustomed to New England habits, who has been educated to revere the Sabbath and respect religion, finds little in a Parisian Sunday congenial with his feelings and tastes. The public squares and pleasure grounds are thronged with people, soldiers are marching in the streets, shops are open, and workmen are employed as usual, and the quiet solemnity of the Sabbath day, as observed in New England, is not known. Walter and Minnie, who at home were accustomed to the utmost circumspection on the Sabbath, were shocked at what they saw and heard. They found it almost impossible to comply with the request of their kind mother to spend the day abroad as religiously as they were accustomed to at home. Whether they kept in their rooms or went out, it was all the same; and their young hearts were often pained at the wanton desecration.

One evening, as they sat conversing with the gentlemen of their party, Walter exclaimed,—

"I must write a letter to my Sunday school teacher. I told him I would."

"Well, why don't you, and not be always talking about it?" chimed in Minnie.

"I must; but I have seen so many things that I don't know what to write about."

"Why don't you tell him what we saw the other Sunday afternoon, when we were out?"

"I guess I will."

So when the gentlemen went out to spend the evening with some friends whom they had found that day, Walter locked the doors, and went to writing, while Minnie threw herself on the lounge, and began to think about home — sweet home. What Walter wrote will be found in the following letters.

Paris, 1858.

Mr. Edwards: —

A conversation I have had with father and Minnie to-night reminded me that I promised to write you a letter during my absence. The long-neglected promise I sit down to fulfil. I have seen so much, that I can hardly tell what will interest you most. My sister suggests that I write you an account of what we saw one Sabbath day in the Champs Elysees, as illustrating Parisian life. You must not think, from the account I give, that I have learned to violate the Sabbath. We were passing through the grounds, and what I saw I could hardly help seeing, and the view has only made me love the New England Sabbath more.

Sunday is the great day for this place; and from two o'clock till midnight these gardens are full of people. I can give you no better idea of them than to describe what I saw on the first Sabbath afternoon I was in Paris. Imagine a spot larger than the Boston public garden, flat and level, well gravelled, and finely shaded with trees of all kinds. Running through the grounds from Place de la Concorde on one side to the Triumphal Arch on the other, is one of the most beautiful drive-ways on the globe. In various parts of the grounds, magnificent fountains are playing in the sun, sending their jets high into the air, and forming rainbows in the spray. The drive-way is full of carriages. I made an estimate, and found that two thousand pass by a given spot in an hour, several abreast sometimes — cabs, hacks, noblemen's carriages, and vehicles of all descriptions. Wandering through the grounds, or sitting on chairs, — iron chairs, let at a cent apiece, — or airing themselves in different ways, are from twenty-five thousand to thirty thousand people. The amusements are very singular and very superficial. There are several pavilions, open in front, with a stand which is all decorated with mottoes, and banners, and flowers. On these stands are gayly dressed girls, and exquisitely furnished young men, who are singing, in operatic style, to all who may come to hear. A rope was stretched around an area one hundred feet square, and within this area are a larger number of chairs and little tables. A liquor house is near at hand, and as soon as any one enters the area and takes a seat at the table, a servant will go and ask what kind of drink is wanted, the person being expected to drink to pay for his seat. Any one can stand outside, in full view of the singers, without paying or drinking. The singers are extravagantly dressed, both as to richness and style, and some of them are very fine singers. There are three or four of these places in full exhibition, in different parts of the grounds.

We pass along and come to a number of wooden ships, which are passing up and down, over and over, round and round, moved by machinery — the machine being a human being hold of a crank. There are a dozen of these in different parts of the grounds, all at work in fandango fashion. Then we come to the wooden horse crank, turned in the same way, and the rider is permitted to go round several times for a sou — one cent. The ships and horses are all gayly decorated with flags.

Then we meet troops of children, boys and girls, with air balls, trundling hoops, and playing at various games. Then we see little mimic theatres, where automaton figures come out and dance, or have a stage play, while a great coarse fellow below does the talking for them. Chairs at a cent a piece are let, and an old woman occasionally passes round the plate to get the coppers. A dozen of these theatres are seen, with about one hundred persons, including priests and soldiers, gathered before each of them. And all through these crowds, men are passing with bright cans of coffee on their backs, which they sell to all who wish that beverage, ringing a bell as they pass from group to group.

Then we move on and find here and there little stalls decorated gayly for the sale of fancy articles, from a prayer book to a jewsharp. As we turn from looking at these, a little carriage with a child in it, drawn by eight goats, crosses our path, the owner of the establishment keeping it company, letting it to parents who wish, by the hour or half hour, to amuse their children by giving them a ride. There are several of these about the grounds.

Then we see a table with gingerbread placed on it; the table being raised, the gingerbread is placed at the edges, the cakes, some larger, some smaller, about two inches apart. Over the table is a revolving shaft. By paying a sou, one can give the swivel a shove, and if the end stops over a piece of cake, the winner can take it; if it stops over a vacant place, the man loses his sou.

Then there are billiard tables where men and women are playing for toys of the value of one or two cents. Sometimes pieces of cake, or a cigar, is the stake. Then there are men pitching quoits; shooting matches, where the shooter uses a wooden gun, and the object to be shot at, a few feet distant, a number of pipes, or a pitcher, or some plaster image. Here are little eating houses, and there machines for weighing people, and lifting machines, and breathing apparatus for the expansion of the lungs.

And thus all over these grounds are these light, foolish amusements, which would satisfy no other people on the face of the earth; and these are engaged in, not by children merely, but by hundreds and thousands of adults, not on one day of the year, but on every Sabbath,

— and almost every day of the year. My heart sickened at the sight of so much frivolity and nonsense.

Now, Mr. Edwards, I would like to have you read this letter to the class, and tell them that though I walked with father through these grounds on a holy day, and saw as much as I have described, I did not entertain any desire to mingle with those sports, for I constantly felt a sensation of pity and sorrow, thinking of Him who said, "Remember the Sabbath day to keep it holy."

WALTER PERCY.

"Min, wake up," said Walter, as he finished his letter.

"Wha — I can't," yawned the child.

"You must."

"Don't plague me, Walter."

"Well, wake up. I have finished my letter, and want to read it to you."

"What letter?"

"To Mr. Edwards."

And Walter commenced reading, but had not proceeded far before Minnie was sound asleep; and he laid aside the sheet, and took another, and commenced a letter to the clergyman of the church where his father attended. We will read it.

Paris, 1858.

Dear Mr. K.: —

I have just finished a letter to my Sabbath school teacher, telling him what I saw one Sabbath afternoon in the Champs Elysees; and as father has gone out and left me at the hotel, I spend a part of the evening in writing to you. I presume it will interest you most, if I tell you how I spend the Sabbath day. I will tell you something about it.

One Sabbath we went to church at the American chapel, in Rue de Berri, a comely little edifice near the Triumphal Arch. Rev. Mr. Seely, an American clergyman, preached an excellent discourse; and we saw among the people present several Americans who came over in the ship with us. We also saw Mr. Mason, the minister of our government; and it seemed good, after being in Paris several days, and hearing so little of our own tongue, to listen to a service conducted in English. Another Sabbath we went to the Oratoire, and heard the famous M. Coquerell, who, though an old man, is very eloquent. I could not understand much of his sermon, but I saw that the people were very attentive. Then we went one day to hear Frederick Monod, whose sweet and gentle tones ring in my ears even now. As we returned from this church, father gave us a long account of Adolphe Monod, the brother of the preacher, who died two years ago, universally lamented by the Protestants of France.

There is much in Paris that I like, and much that I do not like. The intense frivolity of this nation strikes a matter-of-fact traveller with great force. The avocations, pleasures, and gayeties of the inhabitants seem to be so frivolous, that of the most dazzling show one tires in a short time. And yet this is doubtless one of the most beautiful cities in the world, and presents such a contrast to London, that the change seems pleasant. In London the clouds are generally hanging low, the atmosphere filled with smoke and dust, the houses black, the streets narrow, the windings intricate, and the lanes filthy and unclean. Here the skies are bright, the streets clean and wide, the buildings bright and lively looking; the squares, columns, arches, and decorations numerous, and instead of long, winding lanes and avenues, we have the broad, beautiful Boulevards, which stretch all around the city. In London, the plague-breeding Thames frightens the traveller from its bridges, banks, and waves; in Paris, the Seine, blue and rapid, invites the stranger to gaze upon and bathe in its rippling bosom.

But England has the Sabbath and the Anglo-Saxon mind, and I know you would like it better than France. But I am forgetting that you have been in Europe, and know much more than I do about both of these countries. So I need write no more.

WALTER PERCY.

"Now, a little letter to Charlie," said Walter to himself, as he took up a new sheet of paper.

"What did you say about Charlie?" asked Minnie, half awake and half asleep.

"I said I was going to write to him."

"Well, write away. I wish I had the little fellow here."

"So do I! Wouldn't I hug him?"

Walter wrote to his little brother as follows:

LITTLE CHARLIE: —

How are you, my boy? Are you tired of waiting for brother and sister to come home? Well, we shall get back soon, and have a great many things to tell you that will make you stare. We have seen about every thing here, and expect to see the rest before we get back. We have been into palaces and prisons, seen kings and paupers, and have had enough to keep us laughing or crying ever since we left home.

We expect to have an addition to our party when we leave Paris. Colonel Sanborn, of Ohio, with his wife, are here, and wish to travel north with us; so tell mamma that Minnie will have a lady to counsel her. Colonel Sanborn is a fussy old gentleman, who runs to the door or window every time he hears a drum and fife; who says he came over here to see the trainers, and who seems to be a military enthusiast. His wife is like him, keeps her smelling bottle in her hand, and seems to be very conscious of her importance. Minnie, two or three times, has been detected laughing at her curls, and ribbons, and ruffles, and at her fussy ways. The other day we went to the Madeleine church. The service was nearly done when we entered. The church was all occupied by chairs, and these were let. If a person went and sat down, he was expected to pay one sou for it — a sou is one cent. So Mrs. S. crowded herself into a chair, and left the rest of us far in the rear. The man who had the care of the chairs soon saw her. He was a man very small in stature, but very large in dignity. He began to jabber to the old lady in French, and she replied in English. She did not understand him, nor did he understand her; and the faster he talked in one language, the faster she talked to him in another.

"One sou for the chair," he said to her in French.

"No, no, I don't kneel; I'm a Protestant," she replied in English.

"I don't comprehend," he replied, shaking his head.

"I tell you I won't kneel!" she answered, looking daggers at him.

"I will have pay for the chair."

"I won't be imposed upon!"

"One sou."

"Get out of the way!"

"One sou."

"Mercy!" exclaimed the little lady, bounding up with the greatest indignation, and seizing the arm of her husband she hurried from the church, supposing all the time that the official wanted to force her to kneel. This gentleman and lady will go north with us.

And now, Charlie, I presume you are more interested in knowing what we have bought for you. I need not tell you, for a fortnight ago father despatched a large box of articles to Boston, and before my letter gets to you, it will doubtless have arrived, and been opened. There are presents for mother, for aunt Celia, and aunt Sarah, and for some other persons; some stereoscopic views in the bottom of the box, which you must not injure at all. Keep them safe in my writing desk until I return. I hear father and Mr. Tenant, who have been out this evening, stumbling along the passage; so — But I must close abruptly.

WALTER.

The gentlemen gave Walter an account of their evening entertainments, related to him some amusing incidents of Mrs. Sanborn, who seemed quite unfortunate in getting into trouble about the language; and then asked Walter to read the letters he had written. He did so, and when he had finished, Mr. Tenant asked him, —

"Walter, why don't you have your daguerreotype taken on leather, and sent home, as you had one before?"

"Can it be done here?"

"Of course it can. The very art derives its name from a French"—

"Ah, who?"

"Daguerre. After various experiments, he made his art public in this city, in 1839."

"Had no experiments been made before?"

"Yes; in 1770 there were some experiments made by German chemists. For many years previous to the time of Daguerre the action of light on nitrate of silver was known; but he gave the art a degree of perfection that it had not attained, and was pensioned by government."

The next day Walter and Minnie went out and had daguerreotypes taken on cloth, and put in the letter to Charlie; and at night the former wrote in his journal, in reference to the contents of the letters he had sent home, they describing three Sabbath scenes, "My letters looked three ways for Sunday;" and while the happy party pressed on, those letters were on their way to a much-loved distant land towards the setting sun.

Chapter VIII.

VERSAILLES AND THE COUNTRY.

"ONE week more remains for Paris," said Mr. Tenant, one morning, as our friends were sitting at the table in the hotel.

"And what have we to do?" asked Mr. Percy.

"We must ask Walter. What say you, Walter?"

"Well, we have pretty nearly 'done' the city, as some say, and we have all our excursions into the country to make yet."

"True, and I move that we go to Versailles to-day," replied Mr. Tenant.

"I agree," replied Mr. Percy.

"So do I," said Walter.

"So do I," added Minnie, putting down her coffee cup.

"Agreed," said they all.

So, having finished breakfast, they all went to the cars, which start from a very fine depot, nearly new, and were soon on their way to Versailles, that retreat of royalty and art. The ride through the country was delightful, and the whole party were in excellent spirits. On leaving the cars, Colonel Sanborn and lady, who had come on in the same train, joined them, and together they pursued their way to the attraction of the place — the palace. As they went along, Walter said, —

"Mrs. Sanborn, do you know that there are seven miles of pictures in one pile of buildings, and whoever should give two minutes to the examination of each individual work of art, would require eight days to complete his task?"

"O, dear me!" said the lady; "I shall die going through. Why, I feel all tired out already."

Here she stumbled a little against a stone, and launched out into a tirade against the abominable French pavements, declaring that if she was in power at Versailles she would have the streets in better order.

"She would do a good deal — wouldn't she, Walter?" said Minnie, aside; and the laughter that spread over the face of the lad was checked by a stern look from his father.

They reached the palace, and went through the various galleries, and exhausted the day in looking about at the sculpture and paintings.

THE NEW DEPOT.

They noticed that Napoleon figured very conspicuously in many of the paintings. He is seen at the battle of the Pyramids; distributing the cross of the Legion of Honor at Boulogne; making a triumphal entry into Paris; receiving the deputies of the government which proclaimed him emperor; haranguing his army previous to battle; receiving the delegates and keys of the city of Vienna; giving orders before the battle of Austerlitz; having an interview with Francis II.; entering triumphantly into Berlin; bidding adieu to Alexander; being married to Maria Louisa; crossing the Alps over the winding Simplon; guiding his army at St. Bernard; storming the bridge of Lodi; at Marengo, at Wagram, and in a hundred scenes and places calculated to fire the beholder with military enthusiasm.

The children admired the gardens, that are laid out with the most exquisite taste. They saw bowers with bronze groups, water-spouts, cascades, marble grottoes and cool retreats, all executed with the utmost skill.

"What are these?" asked Walter, approaching a group of edifices embowered in the deep foliage.

"The Great and Little Trianon."

"O, yes, I know."

"I don't; so tell me," cried Minnie.

"They are little private residences erected by Louis XIV., as quiet resorts for his friends and favorites."

"With such a great palace as this, I should not think he would want such little houses as these seem to be."

"Almost all kings have their retreats. The Queen of England goes to the Isle of Wight, the court of Frederick William to Potsdam, the present Emperor of France to St. Cloud, and so the old kings used to come here."

In one of the stables near the Trianon, they saw the state carriage of Napoleon III., and Minnie thought it was much more elegant and tasteful than the huge, cumbrous state coach of England. It was first used at the coronation of Charles X., and the original cost and repairs on it amount to more than one hundred thousand dollars.

They had wandered about a long time, and the day was declining, when Mr. Percy said,—

"Children, it is time to return to Paris."

"Well, pa," said the little girl, "let us take one run more through the palace."

"How much time have we, Walter?"

"An hour, sir, before the cars start."

So they walked hastily through the halls and

galleries of the palace. And here they paused in the apartments once occupied by Napoleon, and leaned on the very table at which he once sat. The children were also much affected when they came to the private apartment of Marie Antoinette, and stood at the little door of the private passage, where her faithful guards were cut down by the mob, who had come out to take her to Paris.

As they conversed upon these scenes, Walter said, —

"Minnie, you have often wished you were a queen — what do you think now?"

"I would run the risk," replied the spirited girl.

"I am afraid you might have a hard time, Min," said Mr. Tenant.

"I would try."

"The past would be a dark shadow. I have learned from reliable statistics, that 'of the royal and imperial wives of France, there are but thirteen out of sixty-seven on whose memory there is no dark stain of sorrow or sin. Eleven were divorced; two died by the executioner; nine died very young; seven were soon widowed; three were cruelly treated; three were exiled; three were bad in different degrees of evil; the prisoners and the heart-broken made up the remainder. Twenty, who were buried at St. Denis since the time of Charelmagne, were denied the rest of the grave. Their remains were dragged from the tomb, exposed to the insults of the revolutionary populace, and then flung into a trench, and covered with quicklime.'"

The last place visited was the opera room, where the court are witnesses of operatic performances.

"This is the room where the royal banquet was given to Queen Victoria, on her recent visit to France," said a French gentleman to Mr. Tenant.

"Ah!"

"Yes; and it was decorated with much elegance. The queen, the emperor and empress sat in yonder balcony, and I thought the former looked sad."

"Sad at what?"

"Probably at the idea that she was the sovereign of so plain a people, so much beneath the French in all matters of taste."

Mr. Tenant turned away to conceal a smile.

The party returned to Paris, much pleased with their visit to world-renowned Versailles.

The next day, they all went to Fontainebleau,

the private palace of Napoleon, where he signed the articles of abdication in 1814. This palace is more associated with the great emperor than any other, and a visit to it is delightful. Internally it is like all the palaces of France, a vast series of galleries of painting and sculpture, magnificent apartments, and gorgeous abodes. It was in this palace that Napoleon confined Pope Pius VII., against his will, eighteen months, treating him with the greatest courtesy, yet keeping him in close confinement, and preventing his escape. And here, too, after he had divorced Josephine, did the emperor come and endeavor to be happy with Maria Louisa, whose apartments still remain as when she occupied them. The forest of Fontainebleau, designed as a royal hunting ground, contains forty-two thousand acres, and is sixty-three miles in circumference, partly natural and partly artificial.

Nothing can exceed the interest of this excursion. The country all around is beautiful, and the ride very pleasant. The children, as they rode along, compelled the gentlemen to tell them much that they did not know before about the wonderful man so intimately connected with this place.

Another excursion was to St. Cloud, the summer residence of the present court. The children found the place very delightful; and they also saw Eugenie walking in the garden with her lady attendants. They also went to the famous porcelain manufactory at Sèvres, where elegant articles are made for royal families, and for others who can afford to pay the enormous price. The party were much interested in the manufactory, as well as the rich display of the show rooms. They also went to St. Denis, where are the remains of the Benedictine abbey built by Dagobert I., who was buried there 638, and to many other places of interest in the vicinity of Paris.

They had now been in Paris several weeks, and had worked very hard at sight-seeing. Walter's journal had been growing constantly, and there were many lengthened descriptions recorded there which are not found in these pages. He had written full and detailed accounts of many notable buildings and places as well as men. He had a complete sketch of the Pantheon, that noble edifice, which has in turn been dedicated to science and to God; the Chamber of Deputies, the Palace of Luxembourg, in which are galleries and halls of surpassing splendor; the medical hospitals, which abound, and are of the highest order; the many fine churches, which they visited — St. Vincent de Paul, St. Eustache, and St. Sulpice ; the magnificent Hotel de Ville, the town hall of Paris, rivalling Persian fables in splendor ; the Palace of the Legion of Honor, the Napoleon Barracks, the bridges on the river, the Palace of Justice, the Tower of St. Jaques, the Corn Market, Porte St. Denis, and Porte St. Martin, the Bourse, the Place Vendome, the Fountain of the Innocents, and many other buildings and places.

"I think we had better leave Paris soon," said Mr. Percy, one evening, to his friend Tenant.

"So do I."

"Well, when shall we start ?"

"At your convenience."

"Then we can go to-morrow."

Walter said "well," but Minnie thought she should find no such beautiful places as Paris, and wished to stay another week, but was overruled. The conversation was interrupted by a knock on the door, and a servant entered.

"A letter for Mr. Percy."

"Glad to see it."

"Who is it from, pa?" cried both of the children.

"From home."

"Good, good !"

"Well, get away from my arms, and let me open it."

The seal was broken, and out dropped another letter. The first was from Mrs. Percy, directed to her husband and children. The other was for Minnie, and was thus directed: —

>   *Miss Minni*
>   *Percy*
>   *in   Paris*
>   *at the hotel*
>   *France.*

"Well done," said Minnie; "what ignoramus has written to me now?"

"Open and see."

She tore off the envelope and opened the note, and found a letter printed with a pen. Her eye fell on the signature, — CHARLIE, — and she burst into tears, pressing the word to her lips.

"What a goose!" said Walter; "read your letter, or let me."

"Go off; I'll read."

She read as follows: —

CAMBRIDGE :

Sister Minnie, come home. I am tired of waiting. What are you doing so long, away off so far? Mamma drops a tear on my cheek every night, when she hears me say my prayers — she did not cry when you were at home. I go to school every day, and print on my slate. The teacher says "I do it well"— don't I? We have been down to hingham and hull this summer; but we wanted you, and mother says she would rather be at home. Now do come home, Minnie; I'll never plague you any more — now do. Tell Walter that rover licks my face just as he used to his, and goes to school with me, and makes the boys laugh. I wrote this letter all myself. Rose Thornton helped me spell the words, and Bill Ray put in the stops. Tell Walter I want him to come home — I want him to lick Ed Harris like every thing, for he smashed my kite up this forenoon, when I only made faces at him. Here's Bill just come in to put in the rest of the stops. Don't tell father about Ed Harris.

CHARLIE.

When they had all done laughing at this epistle, Mr. Percy asked, —

"What do you think of your letter, Minnie?"

"O, I think if that is a specimen of your boy there, we had better go home and take care of him."

Mr. Percy then read parts of his own letter, containing a number of facts of interest, and some good advice for the children. "Stay," said the unselfish mother, "as long as the tour can be of any benefit to the health of body or mind of yourself or children. The days pass slowly here, though we find enough to do, and your welcome home will be a warm one."

Chapter IX.

THE BELGIC CAPITAL.

IT was a beautiful day in summer, the birds singing, the flowers shedding their fragrance on the air, and all nature seeming full of joy, that our friends rode out of Paris, through the north of France, into Belgium. The hills were covered with vineyards, and the level country was waving with grain. As they rode along, Minnie exclaimed, —

"See that."

"See what?" asked her father.

"Why, over in that field are hundreds of women at work; and there is one holding a plough."

"Yes; the women do much of the field work here."

"It's too bad! And see those lazy men lying down there in the shade."

"You will find, Minnie," said her father, "that the women of America do far less hard work than those of any other nation. You noticed that in the hotels of London and Paris, responsible posts are occupied by women, and as we travel about on the continent, we shall see much more of this."

"Min, look there," cried Walter.

"What?"

"Look over in that field."

Minnie looked, and saw a woman holding a plough drawn by two cows.

"That is too bad!" she exclaimed, stamping her foot on the car floor, in indignation.

"Don't expend your indignation too fast, Min, for if things go on at this rate, you will see a woman and a cow yoked up together, and a lubberly man driving them."

"If we do, I shall move that we turn back, and go no farther among the barbarians."

"Ah, a smart girl you are. If Mrs. Colonel Sanborn was in this car, you could have some one to help you."

"Well, she ain't, and I'm glad; I'm plagued enough with two men and one boy."

"One b-o-y!" replied Walter, reproachfully.

The cars now stopped, and they found they were at the line between France and Belgium. So they were obliged to get out, and have their passports visaed, and their luggage examined. The custom-house officers, with swords hanging at their sides, were hurrying about;

armed policemen and soldiers were lounging around, and every body seemed to be conscious of the importance of the occasion.

"Walter, what barbarous place have we got into now?"

"Valenciennes, I believe."

"Well, I should think from the number of swords and soldiers, that they anticipated an invasion by the Turks."

Walter laughed.

"There, they have got hold of our baggage; let us follow with the keys."

The baggage was carried into a room, and there opened. The gentlemen also came to look after their bags. Mr. Tenant was the last to open his valise; and when he did so, a little bearded officer put in his hand, stirred up the contents, and finally brought up from the bottom a large bottle of medicine which the owner had procured for emergencies. The liquid was of the color of brandy, and of a hot, smarting taste, and a mouthful was a dreadful infliction.

"What's vat?" asked the official, suspiciously.

"Something for my own use."

"Vat is him?"

"Something to drink."

"Vat you say?"

"Taste and see," said Mr. Tenant, who was

somewhat annoyed by the conduct of the officer, who thought it was brandy, and wanted some.

"*Bon*," (good,) said the man, putting the bottle to his lips.

But he had no sooner done so, than he dropped it with an angry exclamation, and for a few moments he flew about like a crazy man, sputtering and scolding.

"What is the matter?" asked Mr. Tenant.

Again the man sputtered out a whole volume of French words, which to our travellers had no meaning, so rapidly and vehemently were they uttered.

"Served him right," said Mrs. Sanborn, who came up at the moment; "for see how he has tumbled my clean dresses. He ought to drink something."

They were, however, all soon in the cars again, riding on towards Brussels, at which place they arrived about the middle of the afternoon.

"What hotel have you on your list, Walter?" asked his father.

"Hotel Bellevue."

"Hotel Bellevue," said Mr. Percy to the driver, whose hack they had taken; and on they rode, Colonel Sanborn and lady following in another carriage.

They found the hotel to be one of the best they had yet found in Europe, and were soon comfortably situated, in large, airy rooms, having from the windows very fine views; and our travellers unanimously voted that it was well named. On descending to the *table d'hôte*, (the common table,) they found the young ladies, who sat at the first table in the Niagara on her ocean voyage, and soon Minnie was having a fine chat with them. In ten minutes she had told them what she had seen, and how much she had enjoyed herself.

When evening came, our party, with Colonel Sanborn and lady, walked out around the king's palace into the public parks, and through many of the streets. As they stood before the royal palace, the king came out, and rode by them. They uncovered their heads, and the king returned the salutation.

"What is his name, pa?" asked Minnie.

"Leopold."

"Is that all?"

"No — George Christian Frederick Leopold."

"What a name!"

"He is a good king, my child."

"Tell me about him — will you?"

"Well, dear, I do not know much about him. Perhaps Mr. Tenant can tell you."

"What say, Mr. Tenant?"

"All the knowledge I have of him is at your service. You know we told you when we were at Windsor Castle of Princess Charlotte, whose monumental tomb you saw."

"Yes, you said you would tell me, but you have never done it yet."

"Then we have not fulfilled our promise — have we?"

"No."

"Well, let the princess go now. This king was her husband. He is the brother of the Duchess of Kent, and —"

"Who is she?"

"Is it possible that you have forgotten?"

"O, I remember; the mother of Victoria."

"Yes; and this king is the queen's uncle."

"I should think the English people would esteem him on account of the Princess Charlotte."

"They do not esteem him much."

"Why not?"

"When he married the princess, he received a pension from the British government of fifty thousand pounds per annum. The princess lived about a year, and then died, and the English wish him to relinquish the pension; but he will not."

"How long has he been king of the Belgians?"

THE BELGIC CAPITAL.   155

"Since 1831. He was, for a year or two, king of Greece."

"These facts are very interesting, and I will try to remember them. Perhaps I shall know enough to tell Walter something by and by."

"You must learn fast then, Min," replied Walter, who overheard the remark.

"I am learning fast. I feel as if my head would burst with the knowledge I have been crowding into it for the past three months. You put all your knowledge into your journal; I put mine into my head."

"Goody! what a head you must have!"

In walking about Brussels, they found the city to be a miniature Paris, reminding them at every step of the gay, beautiful capital of France. They found the same out-of-door habits, the same *café* system, the same language, and, as far as they could see, the same social habits and customs. As they went into the public pleasure grounds, they found drinking and playing of all kinds; and at bedtime, they all returned to Bellevue, tired and ready to sleep.

The next morning they were up early, and all took breakfast together, Colonel Sanborn and lady being with them at the table. They all agreed to ride out together, Mrs. Sanborn declaring that she did not like the *Bulgians*, and wanted to see all there was of their city in the shortest time possible.

They went first to the Cathedral, a large edifice with considerable attraction, and spent an hour there very profitably. While they were present a religious service was held, and a gorgeous ceremony took place, in which the children were very much interested. A view of this Cathedral will be found on the opposite page. Its massive and elegant towers only indicate the elegance of the interior; and as they came out, Walter lingered after all the rest had passed on, gazing upon the noble proportions of this edifice, erected for the worship of the great God.

They also went to Hotel de Ville, a very old building, with a very high and elaborately-wrought spire, and to many other buildings of note and interest. As they were riding about, Minnie all at once exclaimed,—

"Pa!"

"What, child?"

"Is not this the place where lace is manufactured?"

"This is one place where it is made."

"What, Brussels lace?"

"Yes."

"O, why can't I see it made?"

"You can."

THE CATHEDRAL OF BRUSSELS.

"How?"

"We will go to some lace manufactory, where you can see how it is done."

They rode to the banker, to whom Mr. Percy had letters, who gave them the address of several lace manufacturers, and also letters of introduction to them. They found one of the factories very readily, and entered the exhibition room. A lady who was in attendance was very kind, and gave them all the facilities they wanted for viewing the goods.

"O, what a beautiful shawl!" exclaimed Minnie, as the lady held up an elegant fabric before them.

"It be goot," said the woman.

"What does it cost?"

"Eight hundred francs."

"How much is that, Walter?"

"About one hundred and fifty dollars."

"About! You may well say *about!* You are some way from the exact amount," said Mr. Tenant to the lad.

"What a price!" exclaimed Minnie.

"It be long to make him," said the woman.

"How long did it take to make it?"

"It take *une femme* (one woman) year and half year."

"O, a year and a half!"

"You buy him?"

"No; pa could not afford that."

Leaving the exhibition room, they were taken into the manufactory. In one room they found sixteen girls working lace. Their eyes were red, and their fingers seemed to move wearily and slowly; and our friends looked on with pity.

"Do they work it so?" asked Minnie, drawing close up to Mr. Tenant.

"Yes, dear."

"I do not want to wear Brussels lace any more."

"Why not?"

"Because, whenever I see it, I shall think of these poor girls."

"You will forget this."

"No, never!"

"I used to think," said Mr. Tenant, "that a great profit was made on lace; but when I see how slow and tedious the process of making it is, I wonder that it is sold so low."

They visited several other manufactories of lace, and then returned to the hotel, dined, and made arrangements to visit Waterloo the next day. It was curious to see Walter negotiate with a hack driver, who supposed, as he was trading with a *boy*, he could take the advantage of him. But Walter asked to see the legalized tariff of prices, and held the man to the regulations, which were definite and explicit, as to what a driver should have for a visit to Waterloo. The gentlemen were much amused at the way in which Walter managed the matter, and, when he had made the bargain, complimented him highly on his success in bringing the man to proper terms, and not allowing him to take the advantage of him.

"You have not travelled in vain, Walter," said Mr. Tenant.

"I ought to learn something by what I see," replied the boy.

"Certainly; but some people may travel for years, and not learn enough to get through Europe without being cheated every where."

"They cannot be of the Percy family, I think," chimed in Minnie.

"No, no!" replied Mr. Tenant, laughing.

And so they were provided with a carriage and driver at a reasonable rate.

Chapter X.

THE FIELD OF WATERLOO.

THE children were up early on the morning of the day when they expected to visit Waterloo. Napoleon could hardly have hailed the sun of that morn with more expectation than did our hero and heroine.

"Father, it is daylight," was Minnie's salutation.

"Well, what of it?"

"Why, Walter and I have been up an hour."

"You are not as wise as you might be."

"Why not?"

"Because, as you have a hard and long day's work before you, you should have slept as long as you could."

"But how could I sleep?"

"You could have remained in bed, and not been up disturbing me an hour before sunlight."

"But Waterloo, you know."

"Plague take Waterloo!"

"Plague took it, pa."

"What?"

"Plague took it June 18, 1815, Walter says, and we are going to take it to-day."

"Why, child, how you run on — are you crazy?"

"No, pa; but I guess Walter is, for he was giving orders to an imaginary army in the hall an hour ago, and he has had breakfast on the table a long time — and — and — O, dear, how he acts!"

"Well, I suppose I must get up."

"Of course you must."

"Run out now, daughter."

"Yes, sir; Walter is acting Napoleon down in the hall, and I'll go down and help him. I can be Mrs. Napoleon;" and the happy girl ran out of her father's room, nearly upsetting Mrs. Sanborn, who was passing the door.

"Tut, tut! ba, ba! What a vicious girl you are! You ought to be corrected for a felonious assault."

"I didn't mean to do it, Mrs. Sanborn."

"Yes you did. That is the way children treat grown people now."

"Please forgive me!" said the child, with tears in her eyes. "I would not willingly treat an elderly person with disrespect."

"Tut, tut! don't call me old!"

"No, no, I didn't, please, ma'am."

"Yes you did!"

"Mrs. Sanborn," said a deep voice behind, "you should maintain the dignity of the family name. And as for you, Miss Percy," addressing Minnie, "I shall report you to your father."

Minnie ran back in tears to her father's apartment, and that gentleman, having overheard the whole conversation, smoothed down the soft hair of his daughter, wiped the tears from her eyes, and told her not to mind about the matter, but to be very kind to the lady, when they met again.

After breakfast, the whole party, with the Sanborns, started for Waterloo. The day was very fine, and the ride from Brussels a delightful one. The country was fragrant with the incense that Nature offers to her God, and all were in the most excellent spirits, as in two carriages they rode along.

"Well, Walter," said his father, "you have not told us what bargain you made with this driver."

"I thought I had, sir."

"No. How many miles did he tell you it was to Waterloo?"

"Twelve miles."

"What did he charge you?"

"Twenty-two francs."

"Quite reasonable for so nice a carriage, two good horses, and his own services."

"I thought so."

Just then a man with a wooden leg stumbled out from a house at the wayside, and asked charity. Walter threw him a franc, and Mr. Tenant gave him a small piece of money, for which he seemed very thankful.

"It seems to me there are a great many beggars on this road," said Minnie.

"There is another — a blind man sitting by the roadside."

"Give him some money, Minnie; you did not give the other one any thing," said Walter.

They soon found that the road all the way along was beset by beggars. Some were cripples, some blind, and many of them loathsome, forlorn, pitiable objects. It seems that these beggars creep to the Waterloo road, knowing that many strangers visit the field every day, and as these persons are generally in easy circumstances, the beggars expect to reap a rich harvest. At almost every turn they met some poor creature appealing for aid, and long before they reached Waterloo, the children had given away all their spare change.

When about four miles from the battle field, they began to see the guides, who ran alongside of the carriage, throwing in their cards, and begging for employment. They were neatly dressed with blue frocks, and almost all of them pretended to be the sons of old soldiers.

"Now, Walter," said Mr. Percy, "select a guide for us."

"Well, let me look at them," replied the lad.

"Why don't you take that one?" said Minnie, pointing to an interesting young man who ran along, jabbering in a tongue they could not understand.

"He does not speak plain English."

"Well, that one over on the other side."

"I don't like his eye."

"Fudge! Don't like his eye!"

"There is my man, pa."

"Where?"

"That one. Come here, my good fellow."

The man came, and handed the following card: —

WATERLOO GUIDE.

Sergeant J. MUNDA,

AN ENGLISHMAN,

Late 7th Hussars,

THE ONLY GUIDE

WHO SERVED IN THE BATTLE.

THE FIELD OF WATERLOO. 167

"What do you ask?" said Walter.

"How long do you propose to stay?"

"I cannot tell. We wish your services for the day."

"That will be five francs."

"Cheap enough; climb up with the driver."

The man did so, and they were soon entering the village of Waterloo. They left the carriage and driver at a mean inn, and with Munda went towards the field.

"Now, pa, as we walk along, I want you to tell me about the battle of Waterloo. Walter has told me some things, and I want to know more, so that I shall understand what I see."

"You know when the battle took place."

"Yes; June 18, 1815."

"It is an interesting story, Minnie. On the night before that battle, the English army was encamped on the field, and the officers were enjoying themselves in the city of Brussels. A magnificent ball was held in the capital that night; and just as the assembly was gathering, word was brought to Wellington, who commanded the English army, that Napoleon was approaching. Without informing his officers of the fact, he commanded them to retire from the festivities at an early hour. But in the evening, while the dancing was going on, and mirth and merriment abounded, the intelligence spread that the French were advancing. At once a feeling of seriousness, if not of consternation, spread over the assembly, and the ball soon ended."

"Yes, pa, I remember to have read something about that in the reader at school."

"What did you read?"

"I cannot tell; but I know it was some poetry about 'Belgium's Capital,' and 'a ball,' but what it was I do not remember."

"Walter, do you remember any thing that she refers to?"

"Yes, sir. I think she means Lord Byron's description of the Duchess of Richmond's ball."

"Can you repeat any of it?"

"I'll try, sir.

> 'There was a sound of revelry by night,
>   And Belgium's capital had gathered then
>   Her beauty and her chivalry, and bright
>   The lamps shone o'er fair women and brave men;
>   A thousand hearts beat happily; and when
>   Music arose with its voluptuous swell,
>   Soft eyes looked love to eyes that spoke again,
>   And all went merry as a marriage bell:
> But hush, hark! a deep sound strikes like a rising knell!'"

"Pa, what was that knell?" asked Minnie.

"Can you tell her, Walter?"

"Yes.

'But hark! that heavy sound breaks in once more,
As if the clouds its echo would repeat!
And nearer, closer, deadlier than before!
Arm! arm! It is — it is — the cannon's opening roar!'"

"Good, Walter!" said Mr. Tenant.

"Now, pa, proceed with the battle," added Minnie.

"Let me see — where did I leave off? O, I know. The whole night before the battle, the rain poured down in torrents. The French army was drawn up in front of Hougoumont, and the English fronted on a small county cross road, on higher ground, and in a much more favorable position. On the ground, the guide tells me, it will be easy to see that Napoleon went into the battle under many disadvantages, and exposed to many serious difficulties growing out of the marshy and wet ground on which his forces were stationed. Each army had a considerable reserve force which was to be brought on, and each general knew about the time he should want it. Blucher with the Prussian army, and Grouchy with a tried French force, were held back, to be ready at any moment to turn the tide of battle."

"How many soldiers did Napoleon have?"

"Sixty-seven thousand men, and two hundred and forty pieces of artillery."

"How many had Wellington?"

"About sixty thousand men."

"Did Napoleon really expect to conquer?"

"Yes; the hero entered upon the conflict with the highest hopes. 'The enemy's army,' he said, 'is superior to ours; there are, however, nine chances in our favor to one against us." On the morning of the 18th, Wellington rode over and had a full conference with Blucher, unwilling to trust to a messenger; and that general was made fully aware of the plans which were that day to be carried out. The purpose of Napoleon was to overwhelm the English before the Prussians arrived. Early in the forenoon the terrible engagement commenced, and soon became general along the whole line of both armies. The Chateau of Hougoumont was taken and retaken; the trees in the forest of Hougoumont were riddled with balls, and the two finest armies the world ever saw were engaged in mowing down each other. Napoleon had never fairly tried his skill with an English army, and often during the day expressed his admiration of the noble bearing of the English troops. As the day wore on, the advantage was decidedly with the French. The Duke of Wellington, as if conscious that he could hold out but little longer against the terrible assaults of the French, was heard to say, 'O that Blucher or night would come!' About sundown the Prussians appeared in sight. For a while, neither army knew what the new force was; Wellington believing it to be the advance of the army under the Prussian field marshal, and Napoleon thinking it was Grouchy. The conduct of Grouchy cannot now be explained. He had thirty-eight thousand men under his command. He could hear the cannonading of Waterloo; he had received orders from Napoleon to hurry to the scene, but waited in his encampment, toying with a handful of Prussians, until the fate of France was decided. In Grouchy Napoleon had always placed the most implicit confidence; he had ever found him true, and had no idea of being deserted now. The army under Grouchy knew that they were expected on the field. General Vandamme and others asked permission to advance, but were not allowed to do so. Grouchy doubtless proved a traitor, though most historians have charged him with imbecility, rather than treachery.

"When Napoleon knew that it was the Prussians, instead of the French, that had arrived, and that Grouchy was not at hand, he at once gave up all for lost, but continued fighting like a madman. His great mind could foresee the results of his defeat, and he determined to be victorious or die on the field. His last resource was the famous charge of the French Guard. 'This, gentlemen,' he said to them, as he pointed towards the British lines, ' is the road to Brussels;' and though they knew they were rushing to instantaneous slaughter, they answered with a shout, 'The emperor forever!' which was heard as far as the British lines. But the die was cast, and that noble Guard rolled back biting the dust in agony; and soon the whole French army, wounded and cut to pieces, was flying in disorder from the field. Had Blucher not arrived for another hour, or had Grouchy appeared simultaneously with him, the result of the contest might have been different, and Napoleon might still have been master of the field."

"Do not the results show us that the defeat of Napoleon was for the best?" asked Walter.

"Yes, children, men generally believe it best that Napoleon was defeated, and his stupendous disaster is regarded as a wise act of Providence; but not a few of the greatest and best men of the world have felt that the result of that battle was a misfortune."

"I remember," said Walter, "reading that even Robert Hall, an Englishman, said, 'When I heard of the result of the battle of Waterloo, I felt as if the clock of the world had gone back six ages.'"

They had now reached the field, and passing by the cottage where relics are sold, they stood upon the spot where that dreadful battle was fought.

"This does not look as I thought it would," said Minnie.

"I had no idea formed of the looks of the field," replied Walter.

That the young reader may know how the field looked on the day when our visitors saw it, we give the following extract from Walter's journal:—

"The field of Waterloo, at the present time, presents a unique and singular appearance. A huge mound two hundred feet high, the top of which is reached by a rude flight of steps, is in the centre of the field. This mound is composed of earth taken from the surface of the field, which has been dug down for this purpose several feet. Hence, the huge pyramid is literally composed of bones, skulls, pieces of armor, cannon balls of friends and foes. The pyramid is surmounted by a huge Belgic lion, on a pedestal which reaches to a depth of two hundred and fifteen feet. The circumference of the mound at the base is one thousand six hundred and eighty feet; and the whole structure cost four million francs, and required the labor of two hundred men for four years to build it."

The children climbed up to the top of the mound, although when they reached the summit Minnie was panting for breath. Walter went higher than the rest of the party: he climbed up and sat on the back of the lion, and while there made quite a patriotic speech to those who were on the mound below.

As they stood on the mound the whole field was in view before them, and the guide pointed out to the eager party the noted localities. The situation of the Chateau of Hougoumont, the farm house of Haye Sainte, the position of the respective armies, the spots where notable events occurred, were described with minuteness and accuracy; and they stood for some time gazing in the different directions, and talking over the events of that day of blood. Then they descended the hill, and went to the different places, read inscriptions on the various monuments, and gathered relics of the battle.

"Hallo, what is this?" said Minnie, as she found a piece of bone, which looked like a part of a human arm.

"A bone of some poor fellow who was killed that day," replied Walter.

"Look here, look here — a relic, a relic!" shouted the little girl.

"What now, sis?"

"See here," she said, pointing to a bullet embedded in the bone.

They all gathered around her, and as they examined the partially decomposed bone, the bullet fell out.

"A French bullet," said the guide.

"What makes you think so?" inquired Mr. Percy.

"It is smaller than those used by the English — one third smaller."

"Give it to me, will you, Minnie?" asked Walter.

"No, indeed!"

"I should think you might; you don't care any thing about relics."

"I care about this, and would have you know, Mr. Antiquarian, that I shall keep it."

"How selfish!"

"*Selfish!* I should think I was, indeed. Will you give me your piece of Melrose Abbey, or the old button that the soldier at Greenwich told you was on a coat he wore in the battle of Trafalgar, or those mementoes that you obtained in Paris, or — or — any of the rest?"

"Don't mind, Walter," said Mr. Tenant; "I will cut you a cane in the forest of Hougoumont."

"Thank you, Mr. Tenant. Let Min keep her bullet."

"I think I shall, until I get to Cambridge," was the reply.

Mr. Tenant fulfilled his promise; a stick, that Mr. Percy afterwards had mounted for his son, was cut, and taken away as a relic; besides which several military ornaments were purchased of the guides who had found them, and thus all the members of the party were able to bring away some memento of the battle field.

They then went to the cottage before mentioned, where they saw many articles that had been taken from the field of battle, such as muskets, bayonets, cannon balls, swords, pieces of armor, and many other things, at which they looked with much interest. Some of these things were rusted with blood, and all bore evidence of that strife which changed the fate of nations, and affected the destiny of a whole continent.

Somewhat weary they all retired from the field to the inn, where they found a table set for them, which did not look very inviting.

"What do you charge for dinner?" asked Walter of a servant, who could talk English.

"Five francs — extra for strawberries and cream."

"Whew!"

"Well, if you don't want it, you can leave it!"

"You must remember, Walter, that charges here are high, and travellers are expected to pay an exorbitant sum at such places."

"But look at the table, pa!"

"I see it; cold meat and — and bread."

They sat down and made the best dinner they could under the circumstances, and it must be confessed that Walter's indignation was somewhat reasonable. After dinner they all walked together to the church, filled up with tablets and monuments to the memory of the men who fell on that ensanguined field, and which all travellers visit when at Waterloo. And the visit to the church finished the work of the day.

"Come, driver, 'this is the road to Brussels,' as Napoleon said to his soldiers on the day of battle," said Mr. Percy, pointing in the direction of the city.

"*Oui*," (yes,) replied that responsible personage.

They discharged and paid the guide, entered the carriage, and all the way to Brussels the children were plying the gentlemen with questions about Waterloo, Napoleon, Wellington, and almost every other place and person noted in the campaigns of the great emperor.

"How do you suppose Wellington felt when the battle was over, Minnie?" asked her father.

"He must have felt very nicely, I think."

"Why?" asked Mr. Percy.

"Because he had not only conquered the greatest of generals, but had made a great name for himself."

"Very true; but he hardly would have wished another such battle. He said to Lord Fitzroy that evening, after victory had crowned his efforts, 'I have never fought such a battle, and I trust I shall never fight such another.'"

"That is strange!"

"Not very strange, either. The risks were so great, the contest so severe, the losses so immense, that he did not wish another."

"The next might have resulted differently," added Walter.

"Yes; the English were never fully free from fear of Napoleon until he was dead and buried."

"Do they fear Louis Napoleon?"

"Not much."

"Does he not contemplate an invasion of England?"

"He must be insane if he does."

"But, father," said Walter, "did you not notice when we were in Paris, how bitter the lower classes of the people are towards the English?"

"Yes. There is enough in the real position of the two countries to inflame them against each other. The monuments, triumphal arches, and pillars, that decorate London and Paris, are commemorative, to a considerable extent, of victories over each other; and the military idols of each nation — Bonaparte on the one side, and Wellington on the other — obtained victories, each, which the other can look upon only with feelings of sorrow or hatred."

"I have heard," chimed in Minnie, "that if you mention the word 'Waterloo' to the boys in the streets of Paris, they will grit their teeth, clinch their fists, and tell you that the time is not far distant when that stain will be blotted out, and the injured honor of France vindicated."

"That may be," replied her father; "but as time rolls on, that feeling becomes less and less, and as the nations are brought nearer together, and Christianity exerts a more decided influence, the old hatred will expire."

"And yet I should think, from what I have read," said Walter, "that the emperor does now have, or has had, some intention of invading England."

"Well, he will probably abandon it, as his uncle did."

"A man in Paris told me that one day Louis Napoleon asked one of his most skilful generals whether he could land troops safely at Woolwich."

"What did he mean by that?" asked Minnie.

"Why, whether he could get a French army into England, near enough to the Woolwich arsenal to take it."

"Ah, ha! What did the general say?"

"Yes, sire," was the reply; "I could land them safely, but whether I could embark them again is another question."

"And then what did Napoleon say?"

"He said nothing, but stroked his mustache,

and looked blanker than usual, and turned away, and left the general standing alone."

"He doubtless kept up a vigorous thinking."

"Of course he did."

"Walter," said Minnie, "you have asked me how I supposed Wellington felt after the battle. How do you suppose Bonaparte felt?"

"Bad enough, Min."

"Did he say any thing?"

"Of course he did."

"What?"

"Napoleon left on record many sayings, which show his feelings through the day. Whatever he uttered was caught up."

"Tell me about them."

"When he saw the English army drawn up at Belle Alliance, he clapped his hands with joy, exclaiming, 'At last, then, I have these English in my grasp!'"

"What else did he say?"

"As he saw the beautiful regiment of Scotch Grays forming in the morning, he said, 'How steadily do these troops take their ground! How beautifully they form! Observe those gray horses. Are they not noble troops? Yet in half an hour I shall cut them to pieces.'"

"What more?"

"Still later in the day, when he saw the valor

and desperation of the English, as rank after rank was mowed down, he said, 'What brave troops! It is a pity to destroy them; but I shall beat them at last!'"

"Well, what did he say when he was beaten? That is what I wish to know."

"When he saw that the day was lost to him, he was despairing and desperate. 'We must die here; we must die on the field of battle.' He was determined to sacrifice himself."

"But he did not do it."

"No. Marshal Soult took hold of his horse's bridle and turned him from the foe, telling Napoleon that he would not be killed, but taken prisoner and disgraced. This argument roused the fallen hero."

Thus conversing they rode along the road to Brussels, and reached the hotel, delighted with the pleasures of the day, the children understanding more than they ever did before of the events and details of that fatal battle.

Chapter XI.

VIEWS FROM ANTWERP STEEPLE.

"TO-DAY we leave Brussels," said Mr. Percy to the children one morning.

"All ready, sir," replied Walter.

"Well, get your bags packed up, children; and you, Walter, if you think you can fix the change right, may go to the office and settle the bill for the party."

"I'll do it."

"Make no mistake."

Walter went to the office and looked over the bill, studied out the charges, and at length said,—

"What is that charge?"

"Lights," replied the office man.

"Lights?"

"Yes, candles."

"Six francs for six candles?"

"Yes."

"But we did not burn an inch of the candles."

"You might have used them all; they were yours."

"Well, I suppose I must pay for them."

"Yes."

Walter went thoughtfully to his room, and there sat a few minutes in silence.

"What is the matter, Walter?" said his father.

"Nothing, sir; I was thinking."

"Have you paid the bill?"

"Yes, sir; here it is."

Mr. Percy took the bill and went with it to Mr. Tenant's room, and gave it to that gentleman. While he was gone, Walter took the candles from the sockets, and, rolling them up in a paper, put them in his carpet-bag, saying to himself, "I must not let them cheat me. I paid for the candles, and the man said they were mine. Well, we'll see what will come of it."

The carriage soon came to the door, and they were speedily transported to the cars, *en route* for Antwerp. Against the wishes of the gentlemen, the children had prevailed upon them to take a second-class car, and they found, besides themselves, two ladies and three men. Colonel Sanborn and lady had taken a first-class car.

"Why did you drag us into this car, Minnie?" asked Mr. Tenant.

"Because, if we had taken a first-class car,

we should have had it to ourselves all the way."

"That would have been pleasant."

"No; I want to see the people; there we should have seen none but ourselves."

"We shall see."

Just then the two men took out their pipes and began to puff away at them, and in a moment the car was full of smoke.

"I can't stand this," said Mr. Tenant, lowering one of the windows.

One of the women made a motion expressive of her disapprobation of the act, and muttered some unintelligible jargon; whereupon Mr. Tenant, with his usual courtesy, closed the window. Still the smoke grew more dense, and the air of the car more intolerable.

"This is a second-class car, Minnie," said her father.

"So I see."

"I think you will admit that we are taken in, sis," said Mr. Tenant.

"No, sir, I should say we were being smoked out, instead of taken in."

All but Walter laughed, and he kept his countenance.

"Mr. Tenant," said Minnie.

"What?"

"What do you suppose my sedate, sober brother is thinking about just now?"

All looked at Walter, who did not laugh.

"Perhaps he will tell us," said Mr. Tenant.

"Will you, Walter?"

"I was thinking about tobacco."

"About tobacco? What a subject to think about."

"Yes, about tobacco."

"Well, what about it?"

"I was trying to recall what Byron said of it in 1823."

"Can you tell us, my son?" said Mr. Percy.

"Yes, Walter, tell us," said Mr. Tenant.

"O do, bub," chimed in Minnie.

"He says, if I recollect his words aright,—

> 'Sublime tobacco! which, from east to west,
> Cheers the tar's labor or the Turkman's rest;
> Which on the Moslem's ottoman divides
> His hours, and rivals opium and his brides;
> Magnificent in Stamboul, but less grand,
> Though not less loved, in Wapping on the Strand;
> Divine in hookahs, glorious in a pipe,
> When tipped with amber, mellow, rich, and ripe;
> Like other charmers, wooing the caress,
> More dazzlingly when glaring in full dress,
> Yet thy true lovers more admire by far
> Thy naked beauties — give me a cigar.'"

"How long has tobacco been used, father?" asked the lad.

"When America was discovered, it was found growing there, and used by the Indians."

"As late as the discovery of America, do you say?"

"Yes; and it was introduced into England in 1586, by certain persons who had attempted to settle in Virginia. These carried back to England the filthy weed, and —"

"Tut, tut, tut!" interrupted Mr. Tenant.

"Introduced it among the English, who soon made it an article of merchandise."

"I don't see how they could adopt such a vile thing!" replied Minnie.

"Its use was much opposed at first. Queen Elizabeth prohibited its use in church and at court, though Raleigh, then her favorite, was its patron. Pope Urban VIII. also excommunicated all who used it in church. Its use was also punished in various ways. In Russia a man who used it had his nose cut off; and in Persia it was an offence punishable with death."

"I'm glad that Mr. Tenant did not live in Russia then," said Minnie.

"Thank you, Min. Why?"

"Because we might now be travelling with a man without a nose."

They all laughed at the answer of the little girl.

"Father, what does tobacco derive its name from?" inquired the lad.

"Some have supposed that it derived its name from Tobago, whence were exported large quantities of it; but Humboldt, the great traveller, whom you will probably see at Berlin, has told us something different from that."

"What does he say?"

"That the name is derived from the pipe used by the natives of Hayti, tobacco being the name of it in their language."

"Pa, why do you never smoke?" asked Minnie.

"Because I do not approve of the habit; and I hope Walter will never use the weed in any form."

"But, pa, our minister smokes."

"Yes; but that does not make it right."

"Why does he smoke, then?"

"He contracted the habit in college, and should give it up, as he must see the influence on young men is bad."

"But here is my true-hearted gallant, Mr. Tenant — he smokes."

"Mr. Tenant can answer for himself. Doubtless he would confess that it is a bad habit."

"*Admit*, not confess, friend Percy."

"Well, select your own terms."

"Yes, I shall admit all you say as to the use of tobacco. It is a useless and expensive habit; and from my own experience I would advise Walter never to use the article, or indulge in it in any way whatever."

"You preach better than you practise," said Minnie.

"Perhaps I do; but my preaching on this subject is better than my practice. A large majority of the men who use tobacco will tell Walter as I do — not to use it."

"I do not intend to use tobacco," said Walter; "and yet I would like to know more about the plant."

So Mr. Percy gave the children many interesting particulars in relation to the culture of tobacco, the climates in which it is raised, and the methods of its manufacture, in all of which they were much interested.

At this point Walter, seeing one of the women very much interested in the conversation, said to her, —

"Do you speak English?"

"Ah — O — I speak him some — little bit."

"I am glad to hear that; then we can talk with you. Where do you live?"

"Live? What you call that?"

"Your home — where you stop?"

"Ah, yes; in Antwerp."
"We are going there."
"Ah, yes — goot! You be English?"
"No."
"French?"
"No."
"Dutch?"
"No."
"What language you speak?"
"English."
"And you no English?'
"No."
"What be you?"
"We are Yankees," replied the lad.
"Haw, haw, haw! — haw, haw, haw!"
"What are you laughing at?"
"Haw, haw, haw!"
"What is the matter with you?"
"Haw, haw, haw! you say you be *monkeys*? Haw, haw, haw!"
"Yankees, I said."
"Haw, haw, haw — *monkeys* — monkeys do so," she said, imitating the contortions of the monkey with her face.

The party, perceiving the mistake, began to laugh, and she still repeated, —

"Monkeys! you be monkeys!"

Then she turned to the other persons in the

car, and told them what Walter had said, and they looked at our friends, surveyed them from head to foot, and began to laugh immoderately, which more than ever excited the merriment of the party.

Walter tried to explain; but the more he attempted to explain what a Yankee was, the more the woman laughed.

The lad was touched, and said, "What specimen of monkeys do you suppose we are?"

"Spec-i-*men?* Men not be any monkey at all!"

"Hum! how stupid!" said Minnie to Mr. Tenant, against whose shoulder she was leaning her head.

Thus they rode on to Antwerp, which is a pleasant journey from Brussels, the time on the road being but little over an hour; and so much of interest had occupied them on the way, that they were all surprised when the cars arrived at the destination.

"Have you looked up any hotel here, Walter?" asked his father.

"Yes, sir; there are several good ones, the guide book tells us; but I have fixed on one in particular."

"What one?"

"The St. Antonio."

"Why do you select that?"

"I go by my instincts."

"Well, I know nothing about either of them."

Mr. Tenant had by this time found a carriage, and soon they were in front of the hotel. Two or three servants were standing there. One opened the carriage door, one caught the carpet bags, and a third led the way into the house. They found apartments that suited them, and were soon enjoying themselves, and making their plans to see the place. That evening they went out and wandered around the city, and strolled into the public grounds, the children noticing all they saw. And at night the young folks went to sleep weary with talking, riding, and walking.

The next morning, however, they were up early and ready for the day's work.

"Where first?" asked Walter, as they left the hotel.

"To the steeple," answered Mr. Tenant.

"What steeple?"

"Why, the steeple of the Cathedral of Notre Dame, one of the highest in the world; from which we shall obtain a fine view of the country round about."

"That will be nice!"

And so they went to Notre Dame, and, on paying a small fee, were allowed to go into the steeple. As they went up, the tower seemed all at once to be alive with sounds. The whole party paused, and were almost entranced by the musical echoes that filled the steeple.

"What is it?" said Minnie.

"Bells, bells," answered Walter.

"Where are they?"

"Above us."

Up they went, until they reached the bells.

"What a lot of them!" said the little girl.

"Yes. Ninety-nine of them," added Mr. Percy.

"I remember, father," said Walter, "that you told us something about these bells, when we were in Ireland."

"Yes, I remember. It was one day when we were listening to the bells of Shandon."

"But I don't see ninety-nine of them."

"There are not ninety-nine distinct bells, but ninety-nine hammers that strike the bells in different places, producing a variety of sounds."

"What an immense bell is that one in the middle!"

"Yes, it takes sixteen men to ring it."

The bells now ceased striking, the music of

the chime died away, and our friends went up still higher, until they reached the upper gallery, where a sublime view broke upon their sight. The course of the River Scheldt, the frowning Citadel of Antwerp, and the steeples of Flushing, Breda, and Brussels, were in view.

"Glorious!" cried Mr. Tenant.

"Magnificent!" shouted Minnie.

"How high is this steeple?" asked Walter of his father.

"Four hundred and thirty-six feet and seven inches."

"Is this the highest in the world?"

"No."

"What one is?"

"The spire of Strasburg Minster."

"How high is that?"

"Four hundred and seventy-four feet."

"Does this come next?"

"No; a spire in Vienna is next — thirty feet or more higher than this. Then comes this one."

"What is the highest in America?"

"Trinity, in New York."

"O, yes, that beautiful church in Broadway. How high is that?"

"Two hundred and eighty-four feet."

"Only a little more than half as high as this."

"They are building a Cathedral at Cologne, that will have two spires, which, when completed, will be five hundred feet high."

"Shall we see that Cathedral?"

"Yes."

"But the spires are not finished, you say."

"They are hardly begun. But I want you to take particular notice of this spire. You see it is built in a peculiar manner."

"What do you refer to?"

"Notice, children, that it is not of solid masonry, but bits of stone strung on iron bars, and put together in a curious manner."

"O, yes, I see," replied the lad.

"The spire from top to bottom is deemed a very exquisite piece of workmanship, being the most delicate thing of the kind in the world."

"I remember," said Walter, "of reading that the Emperor Charles V. said that it should be kept in a glass case."

"He did say so; and Napoleon said that it could be compared with nothing but Mechlin lace."

"Rather rough looking lace, I think."

"Yes, viewed from this gallery; but you will see the propriety of the comparison when you are on the ground, and carefully examine the structure from a distance."

They stood in the gallery of the tower for a long time, and among the things remembered long afterwards by the children, very interesting were the views from Antwerp steeple. When they came down, they saw the old draw-well of Quentin Matsys.

"Pray, pa, who was he?" asked the little girl, enthusiastically. "They have so many odd things in this country, that I appear very ignorant."

"Very ignorant!" said Walter, dryly.

"Hold your tongue, saucebox!"

"Couldn't hold it."

"Well, don't charge me with ignorance."

"O, I thought you told the truth when you said you appeared very ignorant."

"I did tell the truth; but I don't want to have it flung in my face, Mr. Impudence."

"There is," said Mr. Percy, "a little history to this thing. You see over the draw-well an elegant iron canopy."

"Yes, yes."

"Well, that was the work of the man I have mentioned. He was a blacksmith, and, falling in love—"

"Hum!" said Minnie.

"With the daughter of a painter—"

"It's growing romantic, Walter," she said, aside.

"He changed his profession to secure her, these being the only terms on which her father would consent to the marriage."

"How did he succeed in the new art?"

"Gradually he became a painter of eminence. He was buried at the foot of the spire. Round at the west door of the Cathedral is a tablet to his memory, with a Latin inscription on it."

"What is the inscription, translated?"

"Something like this, I believe, —

"'Twas love connubial taught the smith to paint.'"

"Bah!—that is pretty stuff to put upon Cathedrals."

"You will find many queer inscriptions on the walls of churches, especially when you get into Italy."

"Well, come; let us enter the Cathedral, and see what we can find there."

"Ah, we are just in time!" exclaimed Mr. Tenant.

"In time for what?" asked Walter.

"To see the masterpiece of Rubens, that the priest yonder is just uncovering."

"What is it?"

"A painting—the 'Descent from the Cross.'"

They all pressed forward to gaze at it, and such was the strange fascination of the picture, that they stood looking at it for some time. They also saw several other pictures of Rubens in this church, around each of which a crowd of persons, strangers in Antwerp, were gathered.

Leaving the Cathedral, they repaired to the old church of the Dominicans, and as they entered, Walter asked, —

"What is there here?"

"We shall see," replied his father.

They soon found that it was a famous picture of Rubens, known as the "Scourging of Christ." The beholder starts back with horror, as the curtain is drawn aside, and the light falls upon the Saviour, with his body all livid with the blows, and sees the inhuman monsters as they tear his flesh with their rods.

Mr. Percy told the children that this church was famous for its wood carvings; the pulpit, stalls, confessionals, and many other things, being exquisitely carved of oak. These carvings were designed and generally executed by monks who had nothing else to employ their time.

"Now, children, I want you to see something outside."

"What?"

"I do not know yet."

"Where is it?"

"We will inquire. Let us move quick."

"Come, Min," cried Walter.

"I am coming."

Soon the whole party were gathered outside, where they found an artificial hill raised against the wall of the church, representing Calvary, and the tomb of Joseph of Arimathea. You enter the gate, and find groups of figures, carved in marble, all around you, while in the centre is an eminence, or mound, with the crucifixion scene upon its summit. Below is the tomb, and within the body of Christ. This work is the conception of a monk, who desired to give as correct a representation of Calvary and the tomb as possible. There is also a representation of purgatory, in the flames of which souls are seen quivering and biting their tongues with pain.

As they turned from the church, and walked along the streets, Walter said to his father,—

"I have heard that this was once a very noted commercial city."

"It was. In the sixteenth century it numbered two hundred thousand inhabitants."

"As large as Boston."

"Yes."

"How many inhabitants are there here now?"

"About ninety thousand."

"How does the commerce of the place compare with what it once was?"

"Very poorly. Twenty-five hundred vessels were sometimes found in the river, loading and unloading. But now the commerce is meagre."

"How are the fortifications?"

"Very extensive and formidable. Napoleon conceived the idea of making Antwerp a famous naval port. He spent ten million dollars to fortify the place, and at St. Helena declared that what he had done was only the beginning of what he intended to do. His purpose was to make this city a prominent port, and so fortify it that it would defend the northern frontier of France, and menace the commerce of the Thames, which is but a few hours' sail distant."

"Father, can you tell me what the name of Antwerp is derived from?"

"No, I cannot."

"I have been trying to make out, in my own mind."

"Perhaps Mr. Tenant can tell."

"Can you, Mr. Tenant?"

"I have heard that it was derived from '*Aen't werf.*'"

"What language are these words in? I never heard them before."

"The Flemish."

"What do they mean?"

"'On the wharf.'"

"Well," said Minnie, "I heard you speaking of 'the quays.' What are they — streets?"

"No; the quays are the wharfs."

"O, I might have known."

"I heard you say something about Rubens, yesterday," remarked Walter; "can you give me any facts about him, father?"

"His career was somewhat public, and you are welcome to all I know about him."

"I should like to hear."

"Where shall I begin?"

"You know, father, — tell me where he was born, educated, and all that."

"He was born in Cologne."

"Why, I thought he was a native of Antwerp."

"No; his father was a sheriff of Antwerp, but during some troublous times he went to Cologne, where Peter Paul, his son, was born."

"Peter Paul — was that his name?" asked Minnie.

"Yes."

"Why didn't they put on Matthew, Mark, Luke, and John?"

"Do stop, Min, and let father tell about him."

"When the times of trouble were over, the family returned to Antwerp; and the lad, showing signs of genius, was well educated, and then put into the school of a painter named Van Oort."

"But Mr. Tenant told me, a few hours ago, that he became a master of his art in the school of Otto — Otto — Somebody."

"Otto Somebody! Ha, ha, ha!" laughed Minnie.

"Otto Venius," said Mr. Percy.

"Yes, sir, that is the name."

"He afterwards went into the studio of Venius, where he made much improvement. He soon came to the notice of Archduke Albert, governor of the Netherlands, who employed him, and at length sent him to Mantua, Madrid, and Rome. From that time his fortune was made. He received many distinguished honors — was knighted in England, and died in 1640."

"How old?"

"Sixty-three years."

"Where are most of his pictures?"

"They are found in Europe, in churches, cathedrals, and galleries of art. Whenever I see any of these pictures, I will point them out to you."

Thus the time in Antwerp was spent profitably, and the place which at first did not promise much of interest proved to be full of interest. As they stood at the door of the hotel one day, a French gentleman said to Mr. Percy, —

"You much like *Anvers?*"

Mr. Percy told him he was pleased with the place. When the man turned away, Minnie said, —

"Pa, that man called this city 'Anvers.'"

"Yes."

"What did he call it so for?"

"The French call it *Anvers.*"

"I have," said Walter, "a sheet of paper with a view of the city, and under the view is the word *Antwerpen.* What does that mean?"

"That is Flemish. The Spaniards call it *Amberes.*"

"Dinner waits for the gentlemen," said a servant, appearing then.

"No," said Walter, "the gentlemen wait for the dinner."

"The dinner shall not wait for the lady," cried Minnie, rushing on before the rest; and soon they were all seated around the table, one of the most happy groups of travellers that could be imagined.

Chapter XII.

FUN IN ROTTERDAM.

ABOUT noon one day, the party took seats in the cars for Holland. The day was very fine, and the whole country around smiled with gladness. About half way from Antwerp to Rotterdam, they crossed the frontier and entered Holland. The examination of luggage and passports was very light; the officers on duty merely looked at the latter, and hastily stamped the former.

"This is something like it," said Mr. Tenant, as he took up his carpet bag and entered the car.

"Like what?" asked Walter.

"Like a civilized country, and like decent people."

"The examinations here are light, certainly."

"Light! light! Our baggage is light! but the officers on the line between France and Belgium pulled every thing to pieces, soiled my clean linen, turned out all my shaving utensils, and left me to tumble them all back into the bag again. I wonder they did not arrest me for having a razor with me, and charge me with taking murderous weapons into the country."

"You can't complain of these people here."

"No; I never complain until forbearance ceases to be a virtue."

All this time the cars were rolling on, leaving custom-house annoyances far behind. At some distance beyond the frontier, the cars were exchanged for a steamer, and a river journey of an hour on the winding Meuse was a refreshing change from the dusty railroad.

"How romantic!"

"What is romantic?" asked Walter of his sister, who uttered the exclamation.

"This river, and our position."

"I don't see any thing very romantic."

"You don't?"

"No, sis."

"Well, I do. Here we are on board a little steamer, not as big as the 'Maid of the Mist,' that we saw at Niagara Falls last summer. We cannot understand what these jabbering people say, and we do not know what plans there may be formed to rob us, and—"

"That is romantic, surely!"

"And then look off—how narrow the stream is! what castles in ruins we have passed! how many windmills there are! and — and — O, dear, how the sun beats down upon my head!"

"In consequence of which you will have a very romantic headache."

"Come, children," said Mr. Percy, "the folks are going down to dinner. You must be hungry by this time."

"Yes, sir," said the lad.

"Yes, sir," cried the little girl.

They went down below, and crowded, with a considerable company of persons in various conditions of life, into a little cabin, and took their seats at the table. The air was close, the appearance of many at the table was offensive; and when the food was brought on, it was any thing but palatable.

"I can't go this," said Mr. Tenant, leaving the table, and paying the steward of the boat four francs as he went out.

Mr. Percy remained with the children, but could not eat any thing.

"Will you have any thing?" said the waiter to him.

"A cup of tea."

"No tea, to-day."

"Coffee, then."

"No coffee, sir."

"A glass of water, then."

"No water — water very hot."

"What have you to drink?"

"Vin, vin, vin!"

"What does he mean by that, pa?" asked Minnie.

"He means that they have nothing to drink but wine."

"Singular that they have no water on board."

"They probably have a plenty of it."

"Then why don't they let you have some?"

"Because, if I drink water, they do not get any pay for it. They want me to use wine, or *vin*, as they call it."

"We must have some drink, pa."

"You shall have. I will get some water by and by, if I am obliged to pay for it."

"Pay for it!"

"Yes, a little silver will bring it fast enough."

"Well, get some now."

"No, wait until after dinner. We shall succeed better when fewer persons are present."

"Father, father!" said Walter.

"What, my son?"

"This meat is bad."

"Don't eat it, then. Take an orange or two, or some other fruit, and when we get to Rotterdam we will have a good dinner."

They soon left the table, glad to get out upon deck, where they could feel a breath of air.

"Guess you have been eating hard," said Mr. Tenant, who was sitting comfortably in the after part of the boat.

"Why, what makes you think so?"

"You look red and hot, as if you had been hard at work. The perspiration stands in great beads upon your forehead."

"You would sweat if you had tried for half an hour to eat tainted meat without a mouthful of tea, coffee, or cold water to wash it down."

Colonel Sanborn and lady now joined them. The former was as dignified, the latter as fussy, as ever. They had been trying to make a dinner, but had succeeded very poorly.

"It's an imposition on travellers!" squeaked Mrs. Sanborn at the top of her voice.

"Wife, you will be overheard," said her husband.

"I don't care if I am. It's outrageous! it's wicked! it's — it's too bad!"

"Hush, Mrs. Sanborn!" said the colonel, gravely.

"I cannot hush! — four francs for such a dinner! One dollar and sixty cents for what you and I ate."

"Hush, wife!"

"It is too bad! And don't you think that impudent servant told me I was taking up as much room at the table as three persons ought to!"

"Ah, that is the rub!" said Minnie to Walter, aside. "I thought there was something besides bad food in the way."

"Yes, yes; let us go forward to the other part of the steamer."

"To the bows, why don't you say?"

"Well, to the bows;" and forward they went.

A sudden turn in the river brings the city of Rotterdam full into view; and soon the whole company were gathered in the bows of the steamer, gazing upon the vision that had so suddenly burst upon them.

"How large a place is Rotterdam?" asked Walter.

"It has about eighty thousand inhabitants, and is in the form of a triangle — so I am told."

They soon landed from the steamer, and, entering a carriage, told the driver to take them to the best hotel in the city; and in a few minutes they found themselves in front of an elegant public house, over the door of which, in large gilt capitals, Walter read aloud the words, "Hotel des Bains."

"What does that mean, bub?"

"I don't know. Can you tell us, Mr. Tenant?"

"This is the New Bath Hotel, said to be a very good one."

They entered, and ordered dinner at once. Mr. Percy, as well as his knowledge of the language would allow, told the servants what was wanted, and invited Colonel Sanborn and lady to dine with them, which invitation was accepted. Toilet duty was attended to, and the travellers gathered in the garden, where a fountain was playing, and flowers were casting their fragrance on the air. Long did they wait, and the evening shadows began to deepen, but they were not called. Colonel Sanborn began to grow more and more impatient every moment. Hunger was seen in his face, and he quickened his step as he strode up and down the gravelled walks. At length, his patience being exhausted, he exclaimed, —

"You have tried to order dinner; I will show you what a military man can do."

"So do, Thomas," said his lady.

"Waiter, waiter!" shouted the colonel.

The waiter was not at hand.

"Waiter, wait-a-r-r!"

"Vot ish that you want?" cried an aston-

FUN IN ROTTERDAM.   211

ished servant, running into the garden, and looking almost as much frightened as if the house was on fire.

"What shall we call you?" asked the colonel.

"Vat ish that?"

"Your name — what is it?"

"Van Pelt."

"Well, Van Pelt, get some dinner for us as quick as possible; we are as hungry as bears;" and the man tried to tell what he wanted.

The servant, with a look of consternation, nodded assent, and hurried away.

"Now," said the colonel, "we shall see how early dinner will be served," and his countenance was covered with smiles.

But they waited and waited; servants came and went; guests were served and departed; and, after a long time, poor Van Pelt announced that dinner was ready, and they hurried to the table, the colonel forgetting the military precision with which he was accustomed to do every thing. But he had no sooner taken his seat, than his face looked black as a thunder cloud at the spectacle that met his gaze. On the table was a pot of weak tea, bread and butter, and a large dish of pickled beans.

All but the unfortunate hero began to laugh; and even his wife, hungry as she was, could not fail to be amused at the ludicrousness of the farce. The colonel was in a rage, and poured out his wrath on the head of the poor servant, who knew so little of English that he had mistaken the order given him. But the more he was stormed at the more placid he became, and at length, looking in the face of the excited man, asked, with a drollery that convulsed with laughter all the others, —

"Vat's der matter mit you?"

This only made the poor man more furious, and Mr. Tenant was obliged to interfere, or the servant might have received severe treatment. No one knew better than this gentleman how to get along with the case. He pacified the colonel, who, on the whole, was really a good man, and gave such orders as soon spread the table with a fine dinner, which was eaten almost silently, as the scene which had just transpired had made all feel any thing but pleasant.

When the colonel and his lady had retired from the table, the servant, who had stood aloof, returned, and seemed very anxious to please the rest of the party. Mr. Tenant said to him, —

"Your friend has gone."

"Yaw! goot, goot! He feels petter pi and pi!"

The children laughed to hear him talk, and

THE CHURCH.

FUN IN ROTTERDAM. 215

Minnie declared that he was a "right down good fellow." The evening was spent in a short walk in the vicinity of the hotel.

In the morning they all went out again to look about the place, and the children were much amused at what they saw. It was some kind of a *fête* day, and the streets were thronged by thousands of people.

"Why, father," said Minnie, "the streets are half of them filled with water."

"Yes," replied the gentleman addressed; "there are as many canals as streets in the city, and it is amusing and odd to see vessels moving along through the city, tall masts passing by the windows of the hotels, and boats scudding along, propelled by the merry boatmen, and churches setting almost in the water."

See engraving on page 213.

"And how do the people cross these canals?"

"Look, and you will see."

"O, yes, I see; bridges are thrown across for foot passengers and travellers."

"I notice," said Mr. Tenant, "there are some peculiarities to the houses not seen elsewhere. The ends of the roof are very peculiar in their construction, and the houses are built so as to hang over into the street two or three feet."

"Yes," said Walter, "they hang over so much

in some of the narrow streets we have passed, as almost to shut out the sunlight."

"Walter, Walter!" cried Minnie.

"What, sis?"

"Do look!"

"Look at what?"

"At those women; instead of having on bonnets, they have brass head-dresses, with horns in them."

"Sure enough!"

Mr. Percy explained that these brass head-dresses were very common, and worn on festival occasions, and sometimes on the Sabbath. They give the wearer a very novel and masculine appearance.

"What strange taste!" added Walter.

"What a contrast, Walter," said his sister, "between those brass ornaments, and horns, and pendants, and the heavy wooden shoes worn on the feet!"

"The whole dress is ridiculous as any thing we have yet seen."

"And look, Walter, at those things on the sides of the houses."

"What things?"

"Those mirrors."

"Yes, the people here seem to keep their looking glasses on the outsides of the houses."

FUN IN ROTTERDAM. 217

"Father, what is that for?"

"In going through almost any town in Holland," said Mr. Percy, in explanation, "you will notice a mirror to almost every window. The object of these mirrors is the same which is accomplished by our bay windows, to see up and down the street. Thus a lady sitting in her room, if the door bell rings, can look in a little mirror, which is so placed as to show who is on the doorstep. If she wishes to see the person, she can go down; if it is a beggar, she can let him ring to his heart's content; and if it is an unwelcome caller, she can direct the maid to say, as some American ladies do, 'Engaged.' She can sit at the window, and, by a glass on the side, see who is in the street below, and the whole length of the sidewalk is full in her view. Sometimes three of these glasses are fixed to one window, one to look up street, one to look down street, and one to see who stands at the door. Some houses have these mirrors to all the front windows, and a very simple yet good arrangement it is."

"I should think it might be," said Walter; "and should the people in some of the long, narrow streets in Boston, where nothing can be seen but a brick wall opposite, have such an arrangement, it would be a great addition to the rooms on the street."

"I don't know. I should hardly wish to see our houses thus fixed out with mirrors."

"There is a statue, pa," said Minnie.

"Yes, I see."

"What is it?"

"The statue of Erasmus."

"Who was he?"

"He was a learned man, and a great theologian. Up to his ninth year he was a poor singing boy in the Cathedral of Utrecht, and from this small beginning he rose to eminence. He died in 1536, and was buried at Bâle, leaving behind him several theological and literary works, and a great name."

"Why was his statue put here?"

"Because he was a native of Rotterdam."

"He was gifted," said Mr. Tenant, adding his word to the conversation, "with great conversational powers; so much so, that it is said that on one occasion, when he visited *incog.* — "

"What does *incog.* mean?"

"*Incognito* is a word for unknown, or in disguise; *incog* is a contraction of it."

"O, yes, I understand — go on."

"When Erasmus visited Sir Thomas More,

then lord chancellor, in disguise, the latter was so struck with the brilliancy of his conversation, that he said, impulsively, 'Who are you? You must be Erasmus, or an evil spirit.'"

In the after part of the day they drove to the house where Erasmus was born, which they found used as a vegetable and flower store. The whole day was occupied in looking about the city; and it was very amusing to see the people stop and look after them, they being recognized as strangers. When they reached the hotel at night, they secured dinner, and then went to their apartments, and spent two or three hours in pleasant, interesting conversation upon the manners of the people, and the things they had seen.

"Don't you think Holland is the strangest country we have yet seen?"

"Yes, there are many queer customs here."

"The country itself is peculiar; I am told that it is lower than the level of the sea."

"Yes, it is so; and the water is kept out by dikes."

"I should think it would sometimes be overflowed."

"There is great danger of it, and nothing but ceaseless vigilance can prevent it."

"What are the dikes made of?"

"They consist of a sort of willow thatch-work, inlaid and overlaid with clay, and need constant repair. It is said that the amount expended every year in dikes, and water levels, and canals, reaches the immense sum of three million dollars."

"Has the country ever been inundated?"

"It has been partially inundated several times."

"Well, how are the canals dug?"

"There is no difficulty with that, as there are windmills all over the country to pump the water out and drain the land. Should an inundation take place, the water would soon be pumped out again."

"I remember what some poet says about this country."

"What is it?"

"As near as I can remember, the lines run as follows: —

> 'A country that draws fifty feet of water,
> In which men live as in the hold of nature,
> And when the sea doth in upon them break,
> And drown a province, does but spring a leak.'"

"You know where that came from, don't you?"

"No, sir."

"The author of Hudibras is responsible for it."

"Who was he?"

"Samuel Butler — a distinguished English poet."

"And I remember some other lines, written by the same poet, upon this country, so open to satire in consequence of its oddities."

"Repeat them, pa; O, do, if they are funny!" cried Minnie, looking up from several views she had that day purchased.

"I will try. Butler speaks of the Dutch as people

> 'Who always ply the pump, and never think
> They can be safe, but at the rate they sink;
> They live as if they had been run aground,
> And when they die are cast away and drowned;
> That dwell in ships like swarms of rats, and prey
> Upon the goods all nations' fleets convey;
> And when their merchants are blown up and cracked,
> Whole towns are cast away in storms and wracked;
> That feed like cannibals on other fishes,
> And serve their cousin germans up in dishes;
> A land that rides at anchor and is moored,
> In which they do not live, but go aboard.'"

"Father, you said some of the customs of this people were very queer. What are they?" inquired Minnie.

"Well, one custom that prevails in some towns is this: if a person is sick, it is common to keep a bulletin on the door, so that those who wish to know how the person is, may not disturb the sick one by the knock or the ring, nor the family by his presence."

"That's curious," remarked Walter.

"What other strange customs have this strange people?"

"When, in some towns, a babe has been born in any family, a silk pin-cushion, covered and fringed with plaited lace, is exposed at the door; the sex of the infant is marked by the color — if a boy *red*, if a girl *white*."

"Why, father, who tells that story?" asked Minnie.

"I do, my child."

"O, yes; but on what authority?"

"No less than the noted maker of the European hand-books — Mr. Murray."

"That is good authority, Mr. Tenant says. But what is the object of putting out this pin-cushion?"

"I give you the exact words of Mr. Murray on the subject. The house which shows in this manner that the number of its inhabitants has been increased, enjoys, by ancient law and custom, various immunities. For a certain number of days, nothing which is likely to disturb a lady who is sick, is allowed to approach it. It is protected from legal executions; no bailiffs dare molest its inmates, and when troops pass it on the march, the drums cease to beat."

"In what towns, father, does this silly custom prevail?"

"In Haarlem and Enckhuysen."

"Is there any other custom that is peculiar?"

"Yes, many of them."

"Do tell what they are."

"The Dutch girls here once a year have a festival, at which they hire sweethearts if they have none of their own. When a person dies here, they send about a man curiously dressed to tell the relatives; and other odd customs prevail, some of which you will see as we go on."

"I begin to see the significance of the expression that old Mr. Howard, who lives near us at home, uses so frequently — 'That beats the Dutch.'"

"Whatever beats the Dutch for oddity must be unique indeed."

"Come, children," said Mr. Percy, "it is time for you to go to bed. You will see enough of Holland before we leave it."

"I am ready to retire," said Walter; "but I never have had enough of any country we have visited yet, and if I should get enough of this, it will be the first. Good night, father."

"Good night, my son."

"Good night, Mr. Tenant."

"Good night, Walter."

The door closed on two retreating forms, the children sleeping in two little bed rooms that led out of the larger room occupied by the gentlemen.

DELFT HAVEN.

Chapter XIII.

Mementos of the Pilgrims.

"Go ahead, conductor," exclaimed Walter, as he saw that official pass the window of the car in which the party had taken seats. The conductor looked up with a smile, and mumbled something in an outlandish tongue, which Walter could not understand.

"Where now, pa?" asked Minnie, as the train started.

"We stop first at Delft."

"What have I heard about that place?"

"I do not know."

"Well, I have heard it mentioned, or have read about it."

"Very likely."

"What is it noted for?"

"Delft-haven was the place from which the Pilgrims sailed to America."

The reader will find one of the last acts of that heroic band before sailing, described in the picture on page 10, and a view of Delft-haven is on page 226.

They soon reached the town, which is only a few miles from Rotterdam. They could stop but a few hours, and were obliged to make the best use of their time. They found the streets narrow and ill-looking, the canals filled with stagnant water, and the people stared at them as if a stranger had never visited the place before. Entering a carriage, they prepared to see all there was to be seen.

"Where do you wish to go?" asked the driver.

"To the Stadthouse first," replied Mr. Percy.

"I wonder what the Stadthouse is?" said Minnie to herself.

"The town hall, I believe," said Walter, overhearing her.

They found the Stadthouse to be an old building with a very curious front, and containing some fine old pictures, though Minnie declared that she did not see much in that building to pay for visiting it.

"Where next, pa?" the little girl asked, as they drove away.

"To the Oude Kerk."

"What is that?"

"I told you."

"Please don't plague me."

"The Old Church we are on our way to — so

called because of its age, and to distinguish it from another here, known as the New Church."

"Have you not seen churches enough yet?"

"No; the churches will be the chief attraction of some places we shall visit."

"Mercy!" exclaimed the child; "see that tower tumbling over!"

"Ha, ha, ha!" was the answer she obtained to the exclamation.

"What do you laugh at?"

"At you, sis."

"What for?"

"For supposing that tower is tumbling down."

"What is the matter with it?"

"It is the leaning tower connected with the old church we are to visit."

They alighted at the foot of the leaning tower, which did, indeed, look as if it was coming over.

"What are you coming here for?" was Minnie's question.

"To see old Van Tromp's monument, father says," replied Walter.

"Who was Van Tromp?"

"I don't know."

"Let us ask Mr. Tenant;" and that gentleman coming up at the moment, she inquired,—

"Mr. Tenant, who was Van Tromp?"

"O, Van Tromp was a Dutch admiral. He swept a Spanish, and then an English, fleet from the face of the waters, and gave the navy of Holland great distinction. The King of France conferred upon him a title of nobility, in consequence of his valor."

"Is this the naval officer who fastened a broom to his mast?" asked Walter.

"Yes, the same."

"What did he do that for?" asked Minnie.

"After having defeated the English fleet in the Downs, he had a broom fastened to the mast of his ship."

"What for?"

"As a sign that he had swept the Channel of English vessels."

"He was a *trump*, wasn't he?"

"He was a brave man."

"How did he die?"

"He was killed on the deck of his vessel in a naval engagement. He died shouting, 'Courage, my boys!'"

"His name was 'Van,' you say?"

"No; his name was Martin Harpertzoon Tromp."

"You called him 'Van.'"

"Yes; Van is a Dutch prefix to a man's

name indicative of some rank, as at home we say John Brown, Esq. The Van often means nothing here, as Esq. does with us. Do you understand?"

"I think I do."

They were now in the church, and standing before Van Tromp's monument, on the base of which is a picture of a naval battle, most exquisitely wrought.

They then went to the New Church, in the public square, which they had no sooner entered than a large, ornate monument was seen, the most conspicuous object in the house.

"Whose monument is that?" asked Walter.

"Van Tromp's, I guess," said Minnie.

"No," replied Mr. Percy; "that is the monument of William I., Prince of Orange."

"Who was he?"

"Perhaps you know that the heir apparent of the Dutch throne bears the title of the 'Prince of Orange,' as the heir apparent of the English throne bears the title of 'Prince of Wales.'"

"I have heard so."

"William I., the heir to the throne of the Netherlands, was a brave man and a hero, who, in the troublous times about the middle of the sixteenth century, contended for the liberties of Holland, that was then overrun by foreigners.

Several attempts were made to assassinate him, and at length his enemies were successful."

"Did they kill him?"

"Yes, after several unsuccessful efforts. Once, when he was at Antwerp, a Spaniard shot him with a pistol; the ball entered his right cheek, destroyed several of his teeth, but did not kill him."

"What did they do with the Spaniard?"

"They slew him on the spot. Afterwards a Spaniard and an Italian tried to kill him, but both were convicted, and one was executed; the other committed suicide."

"How was he assassinated at last?"

"He was here at his palace in Delft, and a young Burgundian shot him."

"What did he do it for?"

"He said that a Franciscan monk persuaded him to do it, promising him, in God's name, eternal life, William being a Protestant."

"But," said Walter, "I see on the monument something about a dog — what is that?"

"Ah, I forgot to tell you about the dog. On one occasion the Spaniards had planned an attack upon him, when his dog, knowing that they were enemies, leaped upon his bed, tore the clothes from him, and aroused his master in season for his escape."

They looked at the monument of Grotius, who was born in Delft; at the tombs of the royal family of Holland, that are in this church; and then went over to see the house where the young prince was assassinated, the spot where the murderer stood, the bullet holes in the wall, the place where the poor man fell, dying, in the arms of his wife.

"Who was his wife?" asked Minnie.

"The daughter of Admiral Coligny."

"What, he who was slain on St. Bartholomew's day?"

"Yes, his daughter. She seemed to have had blood to drink."

"Is there a Prince of Orange now?"

"Yes; a wild young fellow, that report says is betrothed to the English Princess Alice."

"Hum! that little girl betrothed?"

"So it is said."

The party then entered the carriage again, and drove about the town, which they found to be neat and dull, and at the expiration of four hours, took cars for the Hague, where they arrived after a short ride, and at which place they proposed to stop a day or two. This city is one of the most pleasant in Holland, and contains galleries of Dutch art, royal cabinets of curiosities, and many fine buildings, which exhibit art and taste, luxury and wealth. There is at the Hague one of the largest collection of Japan curiosities in the world. Figures in ivory, bronze, metal, and wood, costumes, Japan ware, furniture from their houses, and deities from their temples, weapons of war, and the peaceful instruments of agriculture, and many other things throwing light upon the habits and customs of the people of Japan.

Our travellers took lodgings at a very quiet hotel, and for two days amused themselves by looking about the place. They spent much time in the picture gallery, where they saw a very fine collection of paintings, mostly from Dutch artists; they went to the royal palace of the King of Holland, and were presented to his majesty; they visited the collection of Japan ware, the private collections and cabinets, and saw all they could of interest.

They also rode out to Scheveningen, on the sea shore, where the children were amused with the costumes of the fishwives, and the customs of the fishermen, who were seen drawing their fish over the beach, or launching their boats. The nobility of the Hague often come here and take a fish breakfast, and it forms one of the watering places of the coast.

A little circumstance occurred when they left

the Hague, that unpleasantly affected them. It seems that, on arriving at the hotel, they found no soap on their washstands, and at once ordered it. After the bills had been settled, and the whole party were seated in the carriage, Mrs. Sanborn occupying the back seat, and Walter on the driver's seat, a servant came running out, and crying, —

" Stop, stop ! "

" Hold on ! " cried Mr. Tenant to that personage, who had just started his horses.

" Stop, stop ! " said the servant, out of breath.

" What is the matter now ? "

" You have not paid for the soap."

" The soap ! What soap ? "

" The soap was not put in the bill, sir," said the servant in broken English.

" What soap ? "

" The soap you washed your hands with."

" O, ah ! How much is it ? "

" Four cakes — four francs."

" But we did not use it."

" You washed with it once."

" Well — eighty cents for soap to wash our faces with two or three times."

" They charge that at all hotels in this country."

" Do they ? Then it is extortion."

"Gentlemen should not order it."

"Here is your money," said Mr. Tenant, counting out four francs.

In the mean time, Walter had gone into the hotel, and returned bearing the four cakes of soap.

"They are ours," he said — "we have paid for them."

"Ye-ye-s," said the servant, with a lugubrious grin; and the carriage drove away.

"I don't know about the propriety of your course, Walter," said his father.

"Why not, pa? We buy the soap, and pay for it double the charge made at the stores. It is ours most certainly."

"Perhaps it is."

"Now, the candles we paid for at Brussels we have used ever since, and I have estimated that we have already saved seven dollars on lights, and they are not half gone."

"Walter is right, friend Percy," said Mr. Tenant. "We pay for the articles fully, and we have as much right to take them with us as we should have to take a half dozen oranges that we had ordered to our rooms, and paid for."

"But I do not wish my son to fall into penurious habits."

"It is not an evidence of penuriousness to be economical. True economy would lead Walter to do as he has done, and then he has saved something to be charitable elsewhere."

"Why, father," said the boy, "if we should allow these people to take advantage of us on every occasion, your purse would not be long enough to get us all home again."

"Yes; but I must think this matter over before you repeat the process. I want you to be prudent and economical, but I also want you to be perfectly upright and frank in your dealings. I want you to grow up a generous as well as an economical man. But we will talk about it at another time."

"And then you will confess," added Mr. Tenant, "that the boy is right, and your scruples are wrong."

"Perhaps so."

They were soon at the depot, and on the way to Leyden, at which place they arrived that day at about the hour of noon. It has about forty thousand inhabitants, and is a very pleasant place.

"What is the town noted for?" asked one of the children of Mr. Tenant.

"To all Americans it is associated, like Delft, with imperishable memories of the Pilgrims."

"Did they once live here?"

"Yes; and here the faithful pastor, John Robinson, preached to them those doctrines that they planted at length on the shores of Plymouth Bay."

"What else is it noted for?"

"There are some historical reminiscences of the place."

"Please tell us, and we shall better remember our visit."

"On one occasion,— to give you a single fact, — the town was besieged by the Spaniards, who called on the people to surrender. The military commandant of the place was John Vanderdoes, and he sent word to the Spaniards that he would defend the town at all hazards; and when their provisions were gone, his soldiers would eat their left hands, reserving the right to fight with."

"Noble answer!"

"The town held out four months, and for half of that time bread was not seen. At length the people came to the burgomaster, and urged him to give up."

"Did he do it?"

"No. He said to them, 'Here is my body; tear that to pieces, and eat it, but do not ask me to surrender.'"

"Three cheers for him!" shouted Minnie.

"How did it turn out?" asked Walter.

"A storm came and drove in the waters upon the Spaniards, and drowned so many of them, that the rest were conquered. Help also arrived, provisions came, and the people were saved."

While our friends were in Leyden, they visited the ancient university, the museums, and other objects of interest. The children noticed that the place was all surrounded by windmills, and Walter made a note of it in his journal, as the "windmill town."

"Pa, you seem to be very thoughtful," said Minnie, as Mr. Percy sat looking out of the windows of the hotel, in the latter part of the day.

"I was thinking."

"Of what?"

"Of the Pilgrims."

"O, I don't care any thing about them."

"What of the Pilgrims, pa?" asked Walter.

"I was thinking, that for twelve years they here found an asylum, and enjoyed the liberty of worship; along these streets they walked, gazing on the same heavens; and here they banded together to people an unknown continent, and plant deep in the soil of the new world, the Protestant faith."

About the Pilgrims they conversed until the time arrived for them to take the cars for Amsterdam, the next place on their route, where they soon were, having seen the wonders of Haarlem, among which was the mammoth organ in the great Church of St. Buvon. Mr. Percy gave Walter many interesting facts concerning the history of that strange people, and also told him that the Percy family traced their way directly back to some of that noble band.

Chapter XIV.

THE CITY ON LEGS.

"CITY on legs," said Mr. Tenant, as they approached Amsterdam.

"Why do you call it so?" asked Minnie.

"Because it is built on piles driven into the soft mud."

"What, all the houses, and stores, and churches, built on posts driven into the ground?"

"Almost all of them. The earth into which the piles are driven, and over which the city is built, is nothing but a bog; and the piles reach the hard soil below, or the building will not stand."

"The number of piles must be enormous."

"Yes, you may well judge so when I tell you that the royal palace, a large structure, rests upon over thirteen thousand, six hundred of them. How large, then, the number must be that support a city containing over two hundred thousand inhabitants!"

"Is the city all cut up by canals, as Rotterdam was?"

"Yes, more so. The canals divide it into about one hundred islands; and the canals are spanned by about three hundred bridges."

"I should think the houses would tumble down sometimes, and that the streets would cave through."

"They do. In 1822, an immense warehouse, containing seventy-five thousand hundred weight of corn, sunk down into the mud."

"Are not the people afraid to live there?"

"They do not seem to be, though no heavy burdens are allowed to be carried along the streets for fear of the jar."

"How do they get heavy burdens through the city — into and out of it?"

"By water, through canals."

"How deep are the canals?"

"About ten feet."

"How deep down do they drive the piles?"

"For the heavy buildings, they drive them down seventy or eighty feet."

"Is the city built right on the sea?"

"No; it lies at the confluence of the Amstel and the IJ."

"The Eye, did you say?"

"It is pronounced Eye; but the characters that represent it are IJ."

"Are there carriages in the city?"

"O, yes; and omnibuses, I am told."

They reached the city, and found a hotel, and were soon about wondering at the curious city and the curious people.

"What is there to see here, father?" asked Walter.

"There is not much in-door work to do, I believe. The palaces and galleries of art need not occupy much time. What we want to see most, is the structure of the city, the customs of the people, the ways and modes of life."

"I would like to go into some of these boats on the canals," remarked Mr. Tenant. "I understand the people live in them."

"Yes, pa, let us go into them," cried both of the children at once.

So when they came to some large boats on the canals, they went on board, where they found the family, with their dog, hog, and hens, living as comfortably as persons could under the circumstances. The Dutch are a very neat people, and some of the apartments on board the boats were as tidy as the rooms in the houses on the land, and not a few of the industrious women had flowers growing, and other evidences of taste observable. Walter tried to talk with some of the people, but he was not able to succeed much, and Minnie laughed at him for the uncouth sounds he made.

Leaving the boats, they walked through some of the principal streets, the children asking questions all the way along.

"Where do the people get water, father?"

"Water, water!" interrupted Minnie. "I shouldn't think you would ask such a question as that."

"Why not ask such a question?"

"There is water enough — too much of it. The whole city is cut up with canals, and I should sooner think you would ask where they get dry land to walk on."

"Yes, there is water enough, I see — water to float canal boats on, to extinguish fires, and wash clothes with; but where is the water to drink?"

"Ah, I was not thinking of that; but I suppose they have wells."

"You do?"

"Yes, Master Walter, I do."

"Well, that shows just as much as you know about it."

"Know about it! How you talk! Don't they get water here the same as they do every where else?"

"Not exactly, sis."

"Why not?"

"Because in such a soil it must be difficult, if not impossible, to get it. The water cannot be good for any thing at all here."

"Well, how do they get it?"

"Ah, that is just the question I asked father, when you put your oar into the long-boat of our conversation, and interrupted the answer."

"I'll not say any more, if father will tell us."

"The water," said Mr. Percy, on being appealed to, "is brought from Dunes."

"Where is that?"

"A place near Haarlem."

"How is it brought in?"

"By piles laid through the principal streets, by a company of British capitalists."

"How long since it was first brought in?"

"I do not know — certainly not many years."

"What did they have previously? Did they drink this filthy canal water?"

"No; the water was brought in boats from the River Vecht."

"How far?"

"Twelve miles."

"What kind of boats did they bring it in?"

"A large, heavy barge, called *legger*."

"But how did the people get it?"

"They went and bought it, just as you would go and buy milk."

"Singular!"

"Yes; when the legger arrived, a pump was set in the deck, and the people came until the dirty hold was pumped dry."

"Was it expensive?"

"Yes, very expensive, especially so in the winter, when the canals were frozen. The price at such seasons was often exorbitant."

"I should not like to live in such a country."

"Nor should I."

A peculiar kind of costume worn by a woman attracted Minnie's attention, as she pointed out two persons, a man and a woman, in the street.

"These people dress very much as the Pilgrims did nearly two centuries and a half ago," said Mr. Percy, in reply to a remark of his daughter.

"How did the Pilgrims dress?"

"In a singular costume. These persons are doubtless from the country, where the habits, customs, and dress of the people are less affected by strangers."

On the next page this costume is seen.

"What do strangers have to do with the dress of the Dutch?"

PILGRIM COSTUME.

"Very much. The English and French come here, and give their tastes to the people, and the fashions of those visitors are followed in the large cities, while out in the country, the habits and customs change less, and are more primitive."

A long conversation ensued on the costumes of different nations, some of the statements in which the children could hardly credit.

In the Oude Kerk (old church) they saw the fine organ, which, in the opinion of the Dutch, rivals any other in the world; and as they looked at it, and listened, Walter noted all the particulars in his little book.

"How many stops has it?" he asked.

"Sixty-eight, and three rows of keys."

"Is this as large as the organ we saw at Haarlem?"

"Not quite as large, but said to be as fine toned."

"How many stops has that?"

"Sixty stops, and five thousand pipes."

"Is that the largest?"

"No; the organ at Birmingham is larger, and more full. One at Friburg is also of greater capacity."

"Friburg?" queried Minnie.

"Yes, Friburg, in Switzerland."

"I should think, by this church, that the people here might be very rich."

"They are very rich. Immense wealth is treasured here by these grave, pipe-smoking Dutchmen."

"Are there any Jews here?"

"Yes, one tenth of the whole population are Jews."

"Are they rich?"

"They are said to be."

"Father, is there any thing besides what we have seen, that Amsterdam is famous for?"

"It is a city noted for its benevolent institutions, its schools of art, and the perfection of Dutch life. Any one who would get an idea of Dutch customs could do so here."

"I was told," said Walter, "before coming here, to go and see the Rasp-house. What is that?"

"It is nothing now but a sort of police station."

"What was it formerly? It must have been something, for Mr. Lingard, who was here some years ago, told me not to fail to go there."

"There is a building known as the Rasp-house, I believe. Some years ago it was used to imprison small offenders, but its character is changed."

"Why call it the 'Rasp-house'?"

"Because the prisoners were employed rasping logwood."

"There must have been something else, or he would not have been so particular to have me go there."

"I do not know; perhaps Mr. Tenant can tell."

"Mr. Tenant," said Walter to that gentleman, who was walking on ahead with Minnie, "can you tell me what the Rasp-house was noted for?"

"When a prisoner was confined, he was set to rasping logwood."

"Yes, so father says."

"And if he was ugly, and would not rasp, he was put into a cell, and the water let in upon him, and he was forced to pump to keep from drowning."

"That is a curious punishment."

"It was less as a punishment than to make him work."

"I guess there could be no trouble about his working under those circumstances."

"No, indeed."

While the party were in Holland, they visited all the noted places; went into the boats on the canals, and enjoyed themselves very much. The children enjoyed it all, because every thing was so new, strange, and unlike any thing they had seen in England, France, or Belgium.

Walter had an adventure while in Amsterdam, that caused Minnie to laugh at him. It seems that one afternoon he asked permission to go out and make some little purchases, and was allowed to do so, on his declaration that he knew the city so well that he could find his way about. He went out into one store, and then into another, until he had lost his reckoning; and, on turning to go to the hotel, he took the wrong street, and was soon in a portion of the city with which he was entirely unfamiliar. He tried to find a store where French was spoken, but could not. He asked several men the way to the hotel, but could not make them comprehend what he wanted. The women laughed at him, the children gathered around him, and the men seemed to his excited mind to be of a very desperate kind, and he was very much frightened.

In the mean while, the party at the hotel had become somewhat alarmed at his prolonged absence. One, two, three hours passed away, and he did not come; and leaving Minnie in the care of Mrs. Sanborn, the three gentlemen went out in different directions, agreeing to return in half an hour and report. At the expiration of the time, they all met at the hotel, but no Walter was to be found. Mr. Percy then went to the landlord and procured the assistance of seven or eight trusty servants, all of whom had seen Walter, and would know him again. Just as these servants were about to start out, Walter, pale and tired, came running in, much to the relief of his father and sister.

"Where have you been, Walter?" asked the former.

"I got lost."

"Lost?"

"Yes, sir. I turned into the wrong street, and every turn made it worse. I was sure to come out nowhere."

"You should not have gone so far."

"I couldn't help it. I wanted to find my way back, but the more I tried the more I was lost."

"How did you succeed in finding the way?"

"You know, father, the two volumes of travels you bought me just before we left home."

"Yes."

"They were Colman's Familiar Letters; and in one of them I read that he was once lost in a Dutch city — in Haarlem."

"Well, how did that help you?"

"You shall hear."

"Well, talk on."

"He wanted to get to Leyden that night. His friends and luggage were there, and he had only come down to hear the great organ. In travelling about he lost the way, and did not know how to get to the cars. He tried English, but in vain. He used French with no more success. He attempted German and Italian, of which he knew a little, but all to no purpose. The men laughed, the women pitied him, and the children thought they had found a crazy man. Some thought he was begging cold victuals, and some took him for a drunken man."

"How did he get out of it?"

"I'll tell you."

"I do not see that his dilemma could help you much, only on the principle that misery loves company," said Mr. Percy, laughing.

"You will see that it did. At length, he recollected seeing over the railway station the word *Spoorweg*, which, he thought, might be the Dutch for *railroad station;* so he began to shout, 'Spoorweg! Spoorweg!' and, to his delight, found that, by crying it all along, he was enabled to arrive in season to take the cars for Leyden; and he declared, that he should bless the word 'Spoorweg' all his life."

"Well, what did you do? How did you profit by that?"

"I shouted 'Spoorweg!'"

"You did. What good did that do?"

"It helped me out of my plight. Had it not been for 'spoorweg,' I might have been two miles from here now."

THE DUTCHMAN FISHING.

"But I don't understand."

"Why, you see I know the way from the station to the hotel, and by being directed to the station, I found my way to you."

"Very good; but you must not venture so far away from us again, in these strange cities. You may get into trouble from which you cannot so easily extricate yourself."

"I don't fear it."

"Perhaps you do not fear it; but you are young, rash, and venturesome, and must be careful, or you will have trouble."

"Well, father, I'll try to keep out of trouble."

That night they packed their carpet bags, preparatory to starting away from the country of windmills and canals. A Dutchman who one day sat fishing from his own kitchen door, told Walter that in that little country there were about ten thousand windmills, and that it costs annually millions of dollars to keep them turning; and they visited one large windmill, with sails one hundred feet long, situated just outside of the city on legs, as Walter termed Amsterdam in his journal.

www.ingramcontent.com/pod-product-compliance
Lightning Source LLC
Chambersburg PA
CBHW020758230426
43666CB00007B/751